The
War in Texas

Benjamin Lundy

LITERATURE HOUSE / GREGG PRESS
Upper Saddle River, N. J.

Republished in 1970 by
LITERATURE HOUSE
an imprint of The Gregg Press
121 Pleasant Avenue
Upper Saddle River, N. J. 07458

Standard Book Number—8398-1175-6
Library of Congress Card—70-104522

Printed in United States of America

THE

WAR IN TEXAS;

A

REVIEW OF FACTS AND CIRCUMSTANCES,

SHOWING THAT THIS CONTEST IS

A CRUSADE AGAINST MEXICO,

SET ON FOOT AND SUPPORTED BY

Slaveholders, Land-Speculators, &c.

IN ORDER TO RE-ESTABLISH, EXTEND, AND PERPETUATE

THE SYSTEM OF

SLAVERY AND THE SLAVE TRADE.

[SECOND EDITION, REVISED, AND ENLARGED.]

BY A CITIZEN OF THE UNITED STATES.

PHILADELPHIA:
PRINTED FOR THE PUBLISHERS,
BY MERRIHEW AND GUNN,
No. 7, Carter's Alley.
......
1837.

PREFATORY NOTE.

In preparing a second edition of this work, I have been actuated by the same motive that prompted me, when I first gave an exposition of the true causes of the "Texas Insurrection." The grand deception, practised by Slaveholders and Land-Speculators, still operates upon thousands of honest minds, although the eyes of many have been opened by the publication of facts, &c., relative to the subject.

The first edition of the pamphlet having been soon exhausted, while the demand for it was increasing,—and as the subject upon which it treats is one of the most important that now engages the attention of the citizens of the United States,—I have considered that even a further exposition is called for. With this view, the present edition, revised and much enlarged, is offered to the public. The additions which have been made, will be found highly corroborative of the original statements, generally.

That the work, as now presented to the reader, may have a tendency to throw more light upon the question involving considerations of such momentous import, and induce the honest portion of our citizens to give the subject their immediate attention, in such manner as they may deem consistent with their country's honor and the immutable principles of justice, is the only desire of

THE AUTHOR.

THE WAR IN TEXAS.

It is generally admitted that the war in Texas has assumed a character which must seriously affect both the interests and the honor of this nation. It implicates the conduct of a large number of our citizens, and even the policy and measures of the government are deeply involved in it. The subject, as now presented to our view, is indeed one of vital importance to the people of the United States; and, it particularly invites the attention—the most solemn and deliberate consideration—of all who profess to be guided by the true principles of justice and philanthropy. It is not only to be viewed as a matter of interest, at the present day. The great fundamental principles of universal liberty—the perpetuity of our free republican institutions—the prosperity, the welfare, and the happiness of future generations—are measurably connected with the prospective issue of this fierce and bloody conflict.

But the prime cause and the real objects of this war, are not distinctly understood by a large portion of the honest, disinterested, and well-meaning citizens of the United States. Their means of obtaining correct information upon the subject have been necessarily limited; and many of them have been deceived and misled by the misrepresentations of those concerned in it, and especially by hireling writers for the newspaper press. They have been induced to believe that the inhabitants of Texas were engaged in a legitimate contest for the maintenance of the sacred principles of Liberty, and the natural, inalienable Rights of Man:— whereas, the motives of its instigators, and their chief incentives to action, have been, from the commencement, of a directly opposite character and tendency. *It is susceptible of the clearest demonstration, that the immediate cause and the leading object of this contest originated in a settled design, among the slaveholders of this country, (with land speculators and slave-traders,) to wrest the large and valuable territory of Texas from the Mexican Republic, in order to re-establish the SYSTEM OF SLAVERY; to open a vast and profitable SLAVE-MARKET therein; and, ultimately, to annex it to the United States.* And further, it is evident—nay, it is very generally acknowledged—that the insurrectionists are principally citizens of the United States, who have proceeded thither, *for the purpose* of revolutionizing the country; and that they are dependent upon this nation, for both the physical and pecuniary means, to carry the design into effect. We have a still more important view of the subject. *The Slaveholding Interest is now paramount in the Executive branch of our national government; and its influence operates, indirectly, yet powerfully, through that medium, in favor of this Grand Scheme of Oppression and Tyrannical Usurpation.* Whether the national *Legislature* will join hands with the Executive, and lend its aid to this most unwarrantable, aggressive attempt, will depend on the VOICE OF THE PEOPLE, expressed in their primary assemblies, *by their petitions,* and through the ballot-boxes.

The writer of this has long viewed, with intense anxiety, the clandestine operations of this unhallowed scheme; and frequently warned the public of the danger to be apprehended, in case of its success. He has carefully noted the preparatory arrangements for its consummation—the combination of influence—the concentration of physical power—the organization of various means—and, finally, the undissembled prosecution of it, by overt acts of violence and bloodshed:—and he now stands pledged to prove, by the exhibition of well attested facts and documentary evidence, that the original cause, the principal object, and the nature of the contest, are what he has, above, represented them to be.

To give a correct detail of the plan of operations, adopted by the instigators and fomenters of this Texian war, as well as an exposition of the character and identity of those who have been the active instruments of carrying it into execution, I will commence with a brief historical narration of the settlement of the country by the Anglo-Americans. Their proceedings, in connexion with others, relative to the subject before us, will be duly noticed in the course of my remarks. In the performance of this duty, I shall make use of facts and illustrations, drawn from personal observation, and from numerous documents in my possession.

In reviewing the history of colonization in Texas by the Anglo-Americans, it will appear that the first regular plan adopted, was the privilege granted to Moses Austin, of Missouri, by the Spanish authorities, in the year 1820. Previous to that date, a few persons from the United States had temporarily established themselves in the eastern part of the Province, as Indian traders and unauthorized adventurers. A large tract of country was marked out on the map, and Austin was invested with the privilege of introducing three hundred families of industrious, orderly settlers, professing the

Catholic religion, within a given time.—When he had obtained this grant, or privilege, he returned to Missouri, and proceeded to make the necessary preparations for carrying his colonial enterprise into effect. Before completing his arrangements, however, Moses Austin suddenly died,—and his son, Stephen F. Austin, took the business in his hands, as the legal heir and representative of his father. He soon repaired to Texas, with a considerable number of settlers, the most of whom emigrated from the states of Tennessee, Missouri, and Louisiana. But prior to his obtaining legal possession, or effecting the settlement of the families who accompanied him, the revolution occurred, which annulled the authority of the government, and resulted in the separation of all the Mexican Provinces from the Spanish Crown. The circumstances here referred to, rendered it necessary for Austin to apply to the new Government for a confirmation of his father's grant. This was obtained with little difficulty, in a modified form, and both the contractor and settlers were liberally supplied with lands, gratis, on the condition of occupying them and pledging themselves to be obedient to the laws of the country: yet the settlement of the colony was still restricted and confined to persons of the Catholic persuasion.

During the brief reign of the *Emperor* Iturbide, and the succeeding administrations of the *Federal Government*, Austin proceeded with the settlement of his colony, under the same regulations as before, and procured an extension of privilege to introduce settlers in other parts of Texas. Laws were enacted by the Federal Government, regulating the terms and plans of colonization;—and when the Provinces of Coahuila & Texas were united under a State Government, special regulations were made, by the legislature, in conformity with those of the general Congress, all of which were submitted to by the colonists, and binding on them.* The settlements rapidly progressed, (the terms being extremely liberal,) and Austin succeeded in fulfilling his contracts with the government, relative to the introduction of the number of settlers for which he had stipulated—receiving the *fee simple* of large tracts of land as a reward for his trouble.

The spirit of enterprise, adventure, and *speculation* was now aroused; and divers other persons obtained grants, (the privilege of introducing settlers,) with the view of colonizing the remaining vacant lands in Texas. The most prominent "empresarios" (contractors) were Zavala and Filasola, of Mexico; De Witt, of Missouri; Ross and Leftwitch, of Tennessee; Milam, of Kentucky; Burnet, of Ohio; Thorn, of New York; Wavel and Beales, of England; Cameron, of Scotland; Vehlein, of Germany; M'Mullin, Powers, and Hewitson, of Ireland. All these entered into contracts with the government upon the same principles that Austin

had done.† None of them, however, have succeeded in fulfilling their contracts, except De Witt, and Powers and Hewitson. Some of the others have introduced a part of their settlers; but the most have disposed of their "grants" to joint stock companies, organized for the purpose, in New York and Nashville. These companies are extensively engaged in speculating with said "stock," (and "scrip," which they pass off as preparatory titles to land,) among the credulous, the ignorant, and the unsuspecting, wherever they can find such willing to purchase. In no age or nation, perhaps, have unauthorized and illegal speculations in lands been carried to such extremes as in Texas, within the period of a few years past.‡ The swindling operations in the Yazoo land speculations of Mississippi, were mere child's play in comparison. The government has thus been defrauded, and its liberal munificence abused, by the overweening and reckless spirit of avaricious adventurers. As I have before said, the terms offered by the government to *bona fide settlers*, were of the most liberal nature throughout. They were not only authorized to select large quantities of land, and hold the same, in *fee simple*, on condition of settlement,—but they were also permitted to introduce all articles necessary for their own accommodation, for the space of ten years, free of the customary duties paid by citizens of the Republic.—This, indeed, opened a wide door for smuggling goods into the country, to supply the Indian traders, as well as the native inhabitants. The colonists did not fail to improve the opportunity; and many foreigners took lands, professedly with the view of settlement, and engaged extensively in this illicit traffic. Contraband articles—such as arms, ammunition, &c. for the savage tribes—were also introduced in great quantities whenever the vigilance of the government revenue officers could be eluded. Slaves were likewise taken in and held, in violation of the constitution and laws of the State and the decrees of the General Government.

In this state of things, propositions were made by the government of the United States to that of Mexico, for the purchase of the Texas country, with the view of incorporating it into this Union. The overture was instantly rejected by the Mexican authorities, as they neither possessed the inclination nor the constitutional power to alienate any portion of the territory of the Republic. Many of the newspapers in the United States now teemed with

---

* The Colonization Law of Coahuila & Texas will be inserted, at the conclusion of this article.

† There were several others who obtained "grants" from the State. Grant & Beales, and Soto & Egerton, were of the number: but theirs were located in Coahuila.

‡ Sundry "grants" were also made, by the general government of Mexico, to various persons in the *Territory of Santa Fe*. These were, Dominguez; Wilson & Exter; Royuda & Beales, and Chambers. A large portion of the "grants" made to these persons, as well as those in Coahuila, have been transferred to the companies, as aforesaid, in New York—not a settler having been placed upon any of them, except that of Grant & Beales in Coahuila—and a very few have settled there.

designs; and against the latter, for his ill-digested and *unfortunate* measures. But not feeling themselves yet strong enough to cope with the disposable force of the nation, (the native inhabitants, even in Texas, were almost unanimously opposed to their disorganizing schemes,) they endeavored to suppress their feelings as much as possible, and the tranquillity of the country remained undisturbed. The trial of Austin was protracted, and he continued in durance a period of nearly two years.

Some excitement was produced among the Mexicans by the aforementioned turbulent proceedings of the Texas colonists: but as the latter did not at this period appear disposed to push their measures to further extremes, the excitement at length died away, and friendly feelings towards the foreigners were again entertained by the natives generally. The law enacted by the general Congress, in 1830, prohibiting the migration of citizens of the United States to Texas, was repealed in 1833; and the colonists were again admitted, upon the same liberal terms as before. The Legislature of the State of Coahuila & Texas established the trial by jury; and it also enacted that no persons in the State should be molested on account of their religious profession, be it what it might. The adjoining State of Tamaulipas, likewise guaranteed the freedom of religious opinion by law; and the popular newspaper press, throughout the republic, zealously advocated a change in the Federal Constitution, by which the free exercise of public worship, by all denominations of Christian professors, should be permanently secured.

But the spirit of "nullification" had found its way into the Mexican confederacy. It pervaded several of the "sovereign, independent States;" and occasional attempts at insurrection in various places, were the consequence. This still prevented the Federal government from taking efficient measures to enforce the laws in Texas; and the introduction of slaves,* the unauthorized speculating in lands, and every species of smuggling and contraband trading went on as before mentioned. It was currently reported and generally believed, that even some of the individuals at the head of the State government of Coahuila & Texas were deeply engaged in these illegal land speculations—and that immense tracts had been disposed of by them, in contravention of the Federal regulations. At length the executive

* Even while the Convention, before alluded to, was in session, a slave-trader boldly landed a cargo of slaves in Texas, from Africa, via Cuba. This was such a barefaced violation of the laws of Mexico, and the treaties with other nations, that the Convention felt the necessity of passing a *formal* censure upon the conduct of the slaver. Yet some of the members warmly opposed it! and nothing was done to punish the "pirate," although it was publicly known that he was for a length of time in the country, making sale of his slaves, not far distant from where the Convention met. A short time thereafter, another similar cargo was introduced, and disposed of with like impunity.

authorities of the republic determined to send a few troops into the Texas country, to re-establish the custom-houses, and check the various abuses and violations of law, which had long been and were still so glaringly apparent. At this juncture, also, the Mexicans having become wearied with the disorders arising from the principles of nullification, which had taken deep root in their confederated system, a proposition was submitted for their consideration, to change their form of government to that of a consolidated Republic. Austin was finally liberated, through the clemency of the Federal authorities, and he again left the capital—having pledged himself, it was stated, to use his influence in preserving the political tranquillity of Texas.

In their determination to resist the constituted authorities of the Mexican Republic, the Texas colonists calculated largely on receiving aid from the United States of the North. From the commencement of their settlement in that Province, we must bear in mind, the most of them anticipated its eventual separation from the government of Mexico, and attachment to the Northern Union. This was early resolved on by them, unless indeed other measures could be adopted for the perpetuation of slavery. A full and complete understanding existed between them and the advocates of the system in this country and elsewhere. A very active and extensive private correspondence was kept up for this purpose. Their plans were all deeply laid; and the rejection, by the Mexican government of the proposition to cede the territory in question to the United States, had no other effect than temporarily to frustrate their operations and occasion a modification of their arrangements. A vast combination was then entered into (though not *formally organized*) the ramifications of which may be traced through a great portion of the United States, and some of the British colonies, as well as the Anglo-American settlements in nearly all the north-eastern parts of Mexico. Its immediate object now is the establishment of an "Independent" government in Texas, to promote its grand ulterior designs.

As I have said before, the great land-speculators, in New York and elsewhere, (consisting of individuals and companies) have covered with their "grants" almost the whole area of the unsettled parts of Coahuila & Texas, and of the Territory of Santa Fe. These "grants" will nearly all soon be forfeited, as it will be impossible to introduce a sufficient number of settlers in season to comply with the terms upon which they were issued by the government. A recent act of the State Legislature prohibits the renewal of them in Coahuila & Texas; and no hope is entertained that the general Congress will further tolerate such unlimited schemes of swindling speculation, as they have heretofore facilitated.—The most strenuous exertions are therefore made to throw a population into Texas, that will favor the views of these cormorant speculators; and lands are freely offered as an inducement for the enterprising and daring to emigrate from the United States and other countries. Many such have accepted the invitation, and in numerous instances have taken lands to which they can have no rightful claim whatever, and hold the same in violation of the laws.

In case the Independence of Texas shall be established, all grants and claims, as aforesaid, are legalized, (particularly if the claimants take an active part in the revolution ;) the system of slavery is to be re-established upon a firm *Constitutional* basis ; and every facility will be given to the introduction of slaves from the United States, Cuba, and Africa.* This, it is confidently believed, will afford great opportunities to build up princely fortunes in the *Texian Empire*, by the sale of land, the extended traffic in slaves, &c.

It was not considered sound policy, to declare the Texas country entirely independent of Mexico, while the hope of continuing the Federal form of government existed. The colonists still felt themselves too weak to compete with the power of the republic; and it was doubtful whether the auxiliary force from the United States, which they expected to co-operate with them, would be sufficient to ensure success. Besides, they were somewhat divided in opinion among themselves as to the measures that should be adopted, and the *men* who should be intrusted with the authority to direct the operations of the scheme. The most of those who marshalled as political and military leaders, were upstarts in whom they had little confidence—some of them broken down politicians and mere adventurers from the United States—persons, in fact, of very doubtful character and capacity. When the change in the form of government was proposed, therefore, they declared for the Constitution of 1824, hoping that the native citizens of the State of Coahuila & Texas, as well as those of several contiguous States, would unite with them. This would give them time at least, if successful, to acquire more numerical strength to carry out their main design at a future period. But in the result of these calculations, they were totally disappointed. When it was ascertained that a large majority of the states readily sanctioned the proposition to alter the Constitution, and that every one, except Coahuila & Texas, finally acquiesced, without attempting forcible resistance, the native inhabitants of this State also gave in

their adhesion, or refused to join the colonists in an insurrection.†

Previous to the arrival of Austin in Texas, a small number of troops reached its southern borders under General Cos. The government had not contemplated an open resistance on the part of the colonists to the re-establishment of the custom-houses, the enforcement of the laws, &c , and did not send an adequate number to compel their obedience. But, true to their long-settled determination, they proceeded to arrest the march of the Mexican troops into that part of the country. Austin had visited New Orleans on his way home. There the future plans of operation were concocted. He was accompanied to Texas by some daring adventurers. An army was immediately organized. Mexican revenue cutters were seized, under the charge of pirating upon the commerce of the United States in the Gulf of Mexico.‡ The troops under General Cos were driven into the fort at San Antonio de Bexar. Expeditions were fitted out in various parts of the United States, and auxiliary forces proceeded to the assistance of the colonists, under the guise of emigrant settlers. An agent of the Texas land-speculators in New York was stationed at New Orleans, for the express purpose of forwarding these "emigrants," &c. Austin took the command of the colonial army, but he soon thereafter relinquished the office, leaving the Mexican troops besieged at San Antonio. He never was popular with the turbulent spirits in Texas ; and they now got him out of their way by giving him the appointment of commissioner to procure further aid, both physical and pecuniary, from the United States.

† It has been asserted, that the proposal to change the form of government was made, and enforced, by the usurped authority of the President. This is not true. The measure was recommended by others, sanctioned by the general Congress, and acquiesced in by the Mexican people very generally. The Executive, as in duty bound, merely proceeds to enforce the national will. The Mexicans had become weary of the dissentions arising under the Federal organization. The "nullifiers" of that Republic acted with more spirit than those of our country. When they *resolved* to abrogate the laws of the general government, they frequently essayed to put their threats in execution ; and, in too many instances, blood was shed, before their disputes were settled. In the proposed amendments or alterations of their Constitution, the main essential features of a republican government were preserved ; and as the form was more simple, and easier to be comprehended by the people generally, they hoped for more tranquility and permanent prosperity under it.

‡ The writer of this was travelling in company with a captain of one of the United States revenue cutters at the period here alluded to, who had been stationed on the coast of Louisiana a short time before. There were then loud complaints, in the newspapers, of the negligence of our government in protecting our commerce in the Gulf of Mexico.—The Captain was questioned as to the actual state of things there. He replied as follows : "These complaints proceed altogether from the smugglers. The commanders of vessels whom they denominate *pirates*, are regularly commissioned revenue officers, acting under the authority of the Mexican government. The smuggling gentry are sometimes detected, and their goods, arms, ammunition, &c., taken from them; and then they have the barefaced assurance to call upon our government to protect them in violating the Mexican laws."

* I have heretofore adverted to the fact, that slaves have already been introduced from Africa, by the connivance of the colonists, with perfect impunity. We have recently been informed, through the newspapers, that facilities were given to the commander of a regular slave-trading vessel (clandestinely of course,) to procure supplies at New York, and proceed to his destination. And it has been more than insinuated, that persons in high official stations, deeply engaged in Texas land-speculation, were instrumental in furnishing this slaver with means to prosecute his nefarious enterprise. I have no doubt of the truth of the statement.

It was then "neck or nothing" with the speculators and advocates of slavery. They could not even stand upon the basis of "State sovereignty," as a great majority of the *citizens* of Cohauila & Texas itself had agreed, tacitly at least, to the new order of things.* A fractional part only, and that almost entirely composed of foreigners, were disposed to resist, for any considerable length of time, the decree of the general Congress. A meeting of some of the colonists and adventurers was held, and the incipient steps were taken to proclaim the independence and sovereignty of Texas. It was proposed, in describing the limits, to leave the western boundary undefined, in order that the contemplated new republic might embrace as much of the Mexican territory as could be conquered. The intention of the revolutionists is, to comprehend within its limits a vast extent of country west of Texas proper, viz. parts of Coahuila and the former states of Tamaulipas and Chihuahua, as well as most of the territory of Santa Fe. The "grants" to which I have heretofore alluded cover nearly the total surface of this extensive region, with the exception of those portions of Tamaulipas and Chihuahua, which they have in view. In fact, their object is to extend the bounds of the *Texian Empire* to the Rio Bravo del Norte, at least as high up as its great bend, where it passes through the eastern chain of the Rocky Mountains.

I will now proceed to a brief review of the "Declaration of Independence," recently issued by the Texas colonists.—But I will preface my remarks upon this particular subject, with a statement of the population of Coahuila & Texas, as far as it was correctly ascertained in the year 1832-33, immediately previous to the proposed establishment of an "Independent State" in Texas, under the Mexican Constitution of 1824. This statement is taken from official documents. The municipalities, or districts, named, comprise the population of cities or towns, with the inhabitants contiguous thereto, viz.:

Municipalities.	No. of inhabitants.
Leona Vicario, (formerly Saltillo,)	24,087
Vallalonquin,	3,499
Capellania,	3,576
Parras,	11,941
Visca of Bustamenta,	5,189
Monclova,	5,021
San Francisco and San Miguel de Aguays,	1,005
San Buenaventura,	4,212
Nadadores,	1,984

* We do not learn that more than two native Mexicans of note, have joined the colonists and foreign adventurers, in the present insurrection. These are, Lorenzo de Zavala, and General Mexia. The first is one of the "empresarios" connected with the "Galvezton Bay and Texas Land Company," of New York; and the last was banished from the Republic, I believe, on some charge of a treasonable nature. They are both deeply engaged in the land speculations before alluded to—but neither of them were residents of the State of Coahuila & Texas.

Cienegas,				1,631
Abasole,				1,237
Candela,				2,491
Santa Rosa,				2,334
Guerrero,				1,015
Rosas,				2,122
Nava,				569
Gigedo,				863
Morelos,				616
Allende,				678
Bexar,				1,677
Goliad,				1,439
Austin,				6,186
Nacogdoches,				834
Gonzales, (De Witt's colony,)				466
		Total,		84,672

Of these municipalities, the five last named, only, are in what was originally called the Province of Texas. The population of that of Austin, as well as Gonzales, is wholly composed of foreigners. Those of Nacogdoches, and Goliad, contain a large number of native inhabitants. In that of Bexar there are very few foreigners. The others, likewise, contain none of consequence. But although a correct census of the whole population of Texas had not been taken, and of course the exact number was not officially ascertained, an estimate was made by an agent of the general government, commissioned for the purpose, at the period alluded to. He visited the different settlements, and obtained his information from the most intelligent colonists themselves. According to his calculation, the whole then amounted to 21,000. If we deduct the number of native inhabitants in Bexar, Goliad, and Nacogdoches, (say 3,000,) from this estimate, it will appear that the colonists and other foreigners in Texas, at that time, numbered about 18,000. This, it is presumed, included persons of all colors, and in all conditions, except the uncivilized Indians. We will, however, suppose that the number of foreigners themselves amounted to 20,000. The whole population of the State would thus be about 97,000. It will therefore appear, that the number of the colonists was less than one-fourth of the population: and even of that proportion a moiety, perhaps, had not taken measures to acquire legal title to citizenship. From this view of the state of things it is evident, that if the colonists could not exercise as much influence in the legislation of the State as they wished, there was a reason for it. They had their proportion of representatives in the popular branch of government, and all were governed by the same general laws. If they had sufficient cause of complaint, their views, their objects, and their supposed interests, must have been very different from those of the native inhabitants of the country, to whose government they had voluntarily pledged their allegiance. But I have before stated what their views and objects were, and shall at present merely request the reader to bear the same in mind.

In pointing out some of the gross errors, or the unwarrantaɔle assumptions, in the Declaration of Independence lately promulgated by the colonists, I will endeavor to use as much brevity as the case will permit. Passing over their preamble, our attention is directed to an enumeration of sundry grievances, the first of which is stated as follows:—

"The Mexican government, by its colonization laws, invited and induced the Anglo-American population to colonize its wilderness, under the pledged faith of a written constitution, that they should continue to enjoy that constitutional liberty and republican government to which they had been habituated in the land of their birth, the United States of America. In this expectation they had been cruelly disappointed—as the Mexican nation has acquiesced in the late changes made in the government by Antonio Lopez de Santa Anna;—who having overturned the constitution of this country, now offers us the cruel alternative, either to abandon our homes, acquired by so many privations, or submit to the most intolerable of all tyranny, the combined despotism of the sword and the priesthood."

Here the idea is inculcated, that the Mexican nation solemnly pledged itself to guarantee to the colonists the same form of government that they had been accustomed to in the United States. It is true, that in organizing their government, the Mexicans adopted a plan very similar to our own. But the terms upon which they invited and permitted the settlement of foreigners were, that they must be subject to the regulations which the constituted authorities should from time to time see fit to make. The business of colonizing commenced under the authority of the Spanish Monarchy; it was continued under the Imperial form of government, previous to the establishment of the Federal system; and every change was sanctioned by the colonists, and the declaration of their allegiance renewed, until they conceived the plan and purpose of asserting their "Independence." Their charge against the President, of usurping authority and establishing a military despotism, is not borne out by facts. The change in the form of government was made by the representatives of the people, not by the Executive. The Constitutional Republic still exists; and we have no evidence, that, in this respect, the President exercises any authority save that with which he is invested by the laws.

They proceed to say:—

"It has sacrificed our welfare to the State of Coahuila, by which our interests have been continually depressed through a jealous and partial course of legislation, carried on at a far distant seat of government by a hostile majority in an unknown tongue; and this too, notwithstanding we have petitioned in the humblest terms for the establishment of a separate State government, and have in accordance with the provisions of the national constitution, presented to the general Congress a republican constitution, which was without just cause contemptuously rejected."

This language is very different from that used by the colonists before they took the resolution to set up a government for themselves. That they should be disposed to complain of the transaction of legislative business in the Spanish tongue, is marvellous indeed! Had any one the folly to suppose that the natives would have adopted a foreign language, for the purpose, merely, to accommodate a handful of foreign settlers? As to the "humble terms" in which they preferred their application for the privilege of establishing a State government, and the cause of rejection, I must also refer the reader to my former statements.

Alluding to Austin's imprisonment, they gravely assert:—

"It incarcerated in a dungeon, for a long time, one of our citizens, for no other cause but a zealous endeavor to procure the acceptance of our Constitution and the establishment of a State government."

I will leave it to the decision of every candid reader, whether the attempt to organize a State government, without the consent of the national Congress, and after that body had refused its sanction to the measure, can be fairly construed into a "zealous endeavor *to procure the acceptance*" of the instrument! I have before stated, particularly, the course he pursued in this case, and need not repeat it.

Proceeding with the enumeration of their "grievances," the colonists charge the government, in their Declaration of Independence, as follows:

"It has failed and refused to secure on a firm basis, the right of trial by jury, that palladium of civil liberty, and only safe guarantee for the life, liberty and property of the citizens."

We do not learn that the general government ever officially declared, either by the Constitution or otherwise, that the "trial by jury" would be introduced in their code of laws. Yet the Mexican statesmen have evinced a disposition to establish their institutions upon the most liberal basis that the intelligence of the people and the state of things generally would permit. One of the articles of the Federal Constitution is in these words:—

"160. The judicial power of each state shall be exercised by the tribunals that the Constitution may establish or designate, and all cases, civil or criminal, which appertain to the cognizance of those tribunals, shall be terminated in them to final judgment and execution."

The Spanish colonists had never been familiar with that excellent provision in the English code, the trial by jury: and as a substitute for it, the Mexican Federal Government adopted a system of *Arbitration*, which it was supposed would better comport with the habits and understandings of its citizens, at the period of the organization of the Republic. Regular Courts were established for the prompt transaction of all business connected with the judiciary; and the following articles of the Constitution guarantee the privilege of arbitration as aforesaid.

"155. No suit can be instituted, neither in civil nor criminal cases, for injuries, without [the plaintiff] being able to prove, having legally attempted the means of conciliation."

"156. None can be deprived of the right of terminating his differences by means of arbitrators appointed by each party, whatever may be the situation of the controversy."

It was understood that the States were at liberty to establish the trial by jury, when, in the opinion of the Legislatures, the state of society should warrant it. And by the Constitution of Coahuila & Texas, the principle was recognised. The two following articles of that instrument relate particularly to arbitration and trial by jury:—

"178. Every inhabitant of the state can terminate his differences, be the state of the case what it may, by the medium of arbitrators, or in any other extrajudicial manner; the agreement in this particular shall be religiously observed, and the sentence of the arbitrators executed if the parties who have made the compromise do not reserve the right of appeal."

"192. One of the principal subjects for the attention of Congress, [State Legislature,] shall be to establish in criminal cases, the Trial by Jury, extending it gradually, and even adopting it in civil cases, in proportion as the advantages of this precious institution may be practically developed."

In order to carry out the principle alluded to in the last article here quoted, the Legislature passed an act in the year 1834, (I believe,) instituting the trial by jury, and appointed a gentleman of legal acquirements, formerly a citizen of the United States, one of the judges to carry it into effect. A series of essays, written in the Spanish language, were also published in the newspaper at the seat of the State Government about that time, elucidating the nature and advantages of the trial by jury. Thus we perceive that measures *were* taken—probably as soon as the state of things would admit—to incorporate this institution in the code of laws. And, in the alterations proposed for the Constitution of the Republic, no mention has been made relative to this particular subject. The reader will, therefore, judge with what truth the assertion has been made, that the government "refused" to establish the trial by jury.

One of their grievances is declared to be, that the government " has failed to establish any public system of education," &c. Nations are not " born in a day"—neither can their institutions, when newly modelled, be matured instantaneously. " Public instruction" was considered a measure of paramount importance in defining the powers and duties of the government, and was enumerated with others in the constitutional provisions, but various causes prevented the adoption of a systematic plan of operations. The unsettled state of the country at particular times, and the lawless acts of the colonists themselves, were the principal causes that retarded the establishment of public schools and other seminaries of learning,

as the government proposed, and fully intended to have done.

They further charge the Federal Government with having acted tyrannically, as follows:—

" It has suffered the military commandant stationed among us to exercise arbitrary acts of oppression and tyranny; thus trampling upon the most sacred rights of the citizens, and rendering the military superior to the civil power."

In what respect these "arbitrary acts" have been exercised, is not specified. But, as I have before stated, they themselves refused to carry into effect the laws, or render obedience to the civil authority, in numerous instances; and, of course, the Executive was obliged to resort to the use of military force, to cause the due observance of legislative enactments.

Again, they say:—

" It has dissolved by force of arms the State Congress of Coahuila & Texas, and obliged our representatives to fly for their lives from the seat of government, thus depriving us of the fundamental political right of representation."

But they do not tell us that the State government had previously *nullified* the acts of the general Congress, in the sale of immense tracts of land, contrary to the provisions of the colonization laws. They keep out of view the fact, that it assumed the privilege of selling four hundred leagues, (1,771,200 English acres,) even to foreigners, in direct violation of the Federal statutes—and that one hundred leagues, or more, were actually thus disposed of to the New York land speculators. Even the " provisional government" of Texas, established on the return of Austin from the Mexican capital, declared these proceedings of the state government illegal and void. Instead of being necessitated "to fly for their lives," the members of the Legislature fled (it may rather be presumed) to avoid impeachment, or imprisonment and legal punishment for their misdeeds.

They also assert, that the government "has demanded the surrender of a number of [their] citizens, and ordered military detachments to secure and carry them into the interior for trial, in contempt of the civil authority, and in defiance of the laws and the constitution."

We do not learn, however, that measures of this nature had been adopted, until it had been sufficiently ascertained that the "civil authority" was prostrated, and the laws were wholly disregarded, in that section of the republic, so far as they chose to consider them inconsistent with their views and pretensions. The following charge, too, is gravely preferred:—

" It has made piratical attacks upon our commerce, by commissioning foreign desperadoes, and authorizing them to seize our vessels, and convey the property of our citizens to far distant ports for confiscation."

The Mexican government is yet in its infancy, and has a very small marine.—Of course, it has but few experienced naval commanders. Fo-reigners, in whom the government can repose confidence, are therefore occasionally appoint-ed to the command of its armed vessels. I have before stated that the colonists were ex-tensively engaged in contraband trade, the introduction of slaves, &c. The custom house regulations were completely "nullified" by them, when the Mexican troops were ex pelled in 1832. I believe that not a single revenue establishment was kept up, except in those interior towns where the native popula-tion was numerous. When the government vessels did succeed in capturing those engaged in smuggling, &c., it was necessary to take them to ports guarded by troops, to prevent their being retaken by the smugglers and law-less "desperadoes" among the colonists them-selves, in places where they could effect it with impunity. Possibly, some abuses may have existed under this regulation: but had the colonists consented to aid in the execution of the revenue laws in the Texas ports, such abuses (if there even were any) might have been obviated.

Another apparently serious "grievance" is stated thus:—

"It [the general government] denies us the right of worshipping the Almighty according to the dictates of our consciences—by the support of a national reli-gion, calculated to promote the temporal interests of its human functionaries, rather than the glory of the true and living God."

The institution of an established religion is a grand defect in the organization of the Mexi-can Republic. But this is nothing more than what may be said of the English, and many other European, as well as American govern-ments. The colonists well knew that none but the established religion was ever tolerated, constitutionally, by the Mexican government, when they took the oath of allegiance to it. Many of them formally embraced the predomi-nant faith, were baptized, renewed their mar-riage contracts, &c., according to the rites of the Catholic church. But a disposition very ge-nerally prevailed among the Mexican people, to tolerate the public exercise of all other pro-fessions of the Christian religion; and both Methodists and Presbyterians held their meet-ings, openly, in the colonies, without the least degree of molestation from the government or individuals. Even laws were enacted, by Mexicans, providing for their protection in the enjoyment of their religious privileges. Had they shown a disposition to unite with the na-tive inhabitants in supporting the laws of the country, there can be no doubt that these pri-vileges would eventually have been guaranteed them by permanent constitutional regulations. I omit the notice of sundry items in the list of grievances, set forth by the framers of their "Declaration of Independence," as aforesaid. Many of them are merely incidental to the state of war, in which they have designedly involved themselves. But before I conclude

my remarks, I must ask the attention of the reader to one more important specification, which they dwell on with particular emphasis, viz:—that "the whole nature of their govern-ment has been forcibly changed, without their consent;" (meaning without the consent of the Mexican people at large;) and that their "rulers" have established "a consolidated cen-tral military despotism, in which every interest is disregarded but that of the army and the priesthood," &c.

This sweeping, wholesale assumption is em-bodied in their preamble; but in the sequel, they admit that "the Mexican people have ac-quiesced in" what they are pleased to call "the destruction of their liberty, and the substitu-tion therefore of a military government." A few extracts from the Decree of the general Congress, relating to the proposed changes in the Constitution of the Republic, will throw some light upon this part of our subject, which is so completely involved in gloom by the "Declaration" of these revolutionists. The articles of the Decree aforesaid, from the third to the ninth, read thus:—

"3. The system of government of the nation is a republican, popular, representative one.

4. The exercise of the supreme national power will continue to be divided into Legislative, Executive, and Judicial, which cannot be united in any case nor for any pretext.—There shall be established, more-over, means sufficient to prevent the three powers from transcending the limits of their attributes.

5. The exercise of the legislative power shall re-side in a Congress of the representatives of the na-tion, divided into two Chambers, one of Deputies, and the other of Senators, who shall be elected periodically by the people. The constitutional law will determine the qualifications which the electors and the elected must possess; the time, manner, and form of their elections; the period of the elect; and every thing relative to the essential organization of these two parts of the aforementioned power, and to the circle of their prerogatives.

6. The exercise of the Executive power shall re-side in a President, to be elected indirectly and pe-riodically by the people, a Mexican by birth, whose other circumstances, as well as those of his election, his term of office, his powers and mode of exercising them, will be determined by the constitutional law.

7. The exercise of the Judicial power shall reside in a Supreme Court of Justice, and in the tribunals and judges, which the constitutional law shall esta-blish: their prerogatives, their number, duration, radication, responsibility, and mode of election, the said law will establish.

8. The national territory will be divided into de-partments, upon the basis of population and other conducive circumstances: a constitutional law will detail their number, extent, and subdivisions.

9. For the government of the Departments, there shall be Governors and departmental juntas; these shall be chosen by the people, in the mode and in the number, which the law shall establish; and those shall be appointed periodically, by the supreme ex-ecutive power, on the proposal of the said juntas."

These are the principal leading features of the Constitution proposed for the Mexican Republic, under its new organization. It would seem to bear very little resemblance to a mere system of "military despotism," as the Texas colonial insurrectionists assert! The probability is, that the people will possess as much liberty, be equally as well protected in the enjoyment of their inherent, inalienable rights and privileges ; and also witness more stability in their political institutions, and tranquillity among themselves, under such a form of government, than that of a more complicated system.

When it was proposed to organize a Federal Republican government in Mexico, after the brief reign of the *Emperor* Iturbide, delegates were elected by the people to meet in convention for the purpose. This body was denominated a "Constituent Congress," and was invested with authority to frame a Constitution, in much the same way as did the "Convention" which framed that of the United States of the North. But in providing for future amendments or alterations of the Constitution, which was subsequently adopted by the nation, the calling of such conventions was dispensed with; and the necessary power was delegated to the general Congress, to be exercised, should the state of the country require it, under certain formal rules of proceeding. One of the Articles of the Constitution, granting this authority to the National Congress, is in these words :—

"In order to reform or amend this Constitution or the Constitutive Act, shall be observed, besides the rules prescribed in the foregoing articles, all the requisites provided for the formation of laws, *excepting* the right to make observations granted to the President, in article 106."

The Congress was thus constituted a "Convention," for this especial purpose, entirely *independent of the Executive.* The "right to make observations granted to the President," in the formation of general laws, was the same in principle as that of the *Veto power,* given to the President of this republic. In the case before us, it was withheld. It will therefore appear, that the Mexican Congress was duly authorized to "reform or amend" the national Constitution, when the state of the country should require it. Whether the actual state of things *did* call for it, or not, is a pertinent subject for investigation, before we join the revolutionists in their condemnation of the measure. That body acted upon its constitutional responsibility, and it may be presumed independently of all authority but that of the people, to whom alone the members were amenable for the abuse of their power.

I have previously stated that the principles of "Nullification," as professed by many in this country, had taken deep root, and were often practically exemplified, in the Mexican Confederacy. The Texas colonists, individually, and some of the States, in their "sovereign" capacity, acted them out thoroughly; and not only were the tranquillity and prosperity of the nation thus endangered, but even

the stability of its free institutions, and the permanency of the government, were rendered wholly insecure, and liable to eventual destruction. The more intelligent and reflecting among the Mexican people, were fully sensible of this. They found by an experience of years, that the complicated system of government, adopted by their Anglo-American neighbors, was not sufficiently understood by the mass of their citizens, and consequently not adapted to their state and condition. In considering the proposal for a change in the Constitution, the municipality of Toluca expressed the following views and sentiments:—

"Feeling, therefore, the pressing and imperious necessity of terminating and hereafter preventing the abuses which have frequently been made of power by the authorities of the different States--using it formerly and at present in several of them to the prejudice of the people, with whose happiness (the prime object of all social institutions) they had been entrusted, but which they sacrificed to their own private interests or to disgraceful passions: convinced, also, that it is indispensably necessary to adopt a mode of government more consistent with the establishment of an administration so economical as to repair the poverty, decay, and ruin, to which the profession and complexions of the present system has reduced the country, and so strong as to extricate it from opprobrious and oppressive bankruptcy; to supply our internal wants, and restore and consolidate our impaired credit; opposed also to tyrannical and absolute power, whether exercised by one or more persons, or by the unbiassed multitude; tired of enduring sometimes heavy and barbarous oppression, sometimes dreadful and bloody anarchy; desirous at length to see perpetually and irrevocably secured the peaceable enjoyment of a moderate national and constitutional freedom, and of the other social rights which have hitherto been merely nominal, and basely violated," &c. &c.

With this understanding of their state and condition, and this desire to improve it, in order to secure the peace and happiness of themselves and the successive generations of their posterity, the change in the constitution was proposed, and sanctioned voluntarily by an immense majority of the Mexican people. It was also finally "acquiesced in" by them *unanimously,* with the exception of a small fractional part of the inhabitants of one of the states—and that fractional part composed almost entirely of foreigners, many of whom had not acquired citizenship in the Republic. This is the *ostensible pretext,* (though not the real one,) now urged by the Texas insurrectionists, for waging war against the Mexican government. They did not pretend to have sufficient cause of complaint, to adopt measures for their entire independence, so long as the hope existed that the Federal form of government could be continued. It is evident, therefore, that *they* were not oppressed. But they deny to the great mass of the Mexican people the right to abrogate such institutions as their own experience teaches them are unsuited to their condition ; unless, indeed, they will give up a large portion of their country, and leave a great number of their brethren to the exclusive control and unapproved government of foreigners. Texas never did exercise the authority of an independent sovereignty. Neither did the colonists ever, exclusively, possess the attributes of a community, clothed with any political power whatever. When they settled in the country, they took up their abode among the native inhabitants, promised obedience to their laws, and were ever *legally* subject to all the regulations of their government. They never possessed a shadow of legal title to a foot of the soil, further than what a part of them acquired by the munificence and liberality of that same people and government, and what they obtained by purchase from them. What authority then can they claim, to dictate to the Mexican nation the formula of its political institutions—or demand the relinquishment of its right to possess and govern the country in which they have thus been permitted to settle themselves ? It was an acknowledged axiom with the founders of this Republic, that whenever any form of government fails to secure to its citizens generally the possession of their inalienable privileges, in the " pursuit of happiness," &c.—" it is the right of the people to alter or abolish it, and to institute a new government, laying its foundation on such principles, and organizing its powers in such form, as to them shall seem most likely to effect their safety and happiness." Yet they never promulgated the doctrine, that a small minority in a community should exercise the right to prevent the *majority* from carrying this principle into effect. To elucidate the subject more fully, let us suppose a case, which would be strictly analogous to the one before us.

At the close of the American revolution, and prevous to the organization of our present form of government, a part of the Province of Pennsylvania was settled by a considerable number of Germans. They had migrated from the monarchical principalities of Europe, or at least from countries whose political institutions were different in their principles and organic structure from ours. We will suppose they did not approve the democratic republican form of government which our fathers established under the present Constitution. They composed a small part of the population of the province. They were settled among the native inhabitants, (or there were a large number of natives in the same part with themselves) whose ancestors had opened farms and built up villages long before these foreigners had asked or obtained permission to fix their residence there. They had declared allegiance to the government under the first confederation ; they promised obedience to the laws and regulations which should in future be enacted by the legal authorities; and they were kindly treated, and in a few instances advanced to stations of honor, trust, and profit. But although the native inhabitants

in the province out-numbered them, as more than three or four to one, we will assume that they refused their sanction to the government, under the federal organization of this Union. The natives were almost unanimous in giving their assent ; all, except these *foreigners*, approved or finally " acquiesced" in the proposed change.

Now, let us suppose, that in this state of things, these Germans had declared for the old confederation, taken up arms to resist the authority of the general Congress, called upon their brethren in Europe to aid them in their *rebellion*, and finally declared the independence of Lancaster, Berks, and as many other contiguous counties as they might eventually be able to conquer : nay, suppose they had expressed the intention in their " Declaration," to make themselves masters of the whole State of Pennsylvania, a part of Virginia and of Ohio, and nearly all the Territory of Michigan, while they were still dependent upon the Germans in Europe for men, money, and other means to accomplish their object ! ! What, I ask, would the people of the United States have said and *done ?* What would their brethren, " their own countrymen" in Europe, consider their duty in such a case ? What judgment, indeed, would the nations of the civilized world have pronounced upon *their* daring " usurpation" of power—their ambitious, yet impotent efforts--their total disregard of justice, or their ignorance of the fundamental principles of human government? I need not say what the impartial verdict would have been.

Tell me not, that the comparison here fails in the application to our subject. It is strictly correct in every essential particular. If there is any variance in the similitude, the Germans of Pennsylvania would have been more justifiable than the Texas colonists in raising the standard of revolt, had they objected to the change in the form of government upon the principle above stated. Many of the former settled in the country long before the native inhabitants threw off the shackles of foreign domination, and helped to fight the battles of national liberty. But the latter (with the exception of a very few) introduced themselves after the independence of the nation had been secured, by the establishment of a new government. Those who are acquainted with the history of Texas colonization, well know that I have fairly stated facts and circumstances ; and it will be found, in the end, that my inferences are just and my conclusions undeniable.

I have stated that " a vast combination was entered into, (though not formally organized,") having in view the re-establishment of slavery in the Texas country, &c. I might rest the assertion on the evidence already adduced in proof of this; but, in order to illustrate it more clearly, I will ask the reader's attention to some more facts and observations connected with the subject.

This design was openly manifested a short time after the settlement of the famous " Missouri Question," by which it was decided that slavery should never be extended to any portion of the territory of the United States, above the line of 36 degrees and 30 minutes of north latitude. When the treaty, defining the western boundary of Louisiana, was ratified by our government, many of our citizens were dissatisfied, because the Texas country was not included within its limits. To some of these the question of slavery, in that region, did not probably then occur; but soon after the colonization commenced, under Austin, it became a subject of general conversation and newspaper remark, in our Southern States. All the writers for the papers, at that period, contemplated the annexation of the territory to that of the United States. Among the first who publicly advocated the measure, particularly in reference to the extension of the system of slavery, were the writers of two or more series of essays, originally published at St. Louis, in Missouri, over the signatures of " *Americanus*," and " *La Salle.*"* These essays were attributed to the pen of the Hon. T. H. Benton, now a Senator in the Congress of the United States. To give the reader a correct idea of their drift, and the manner in which the doctrines they inculcated were received in different parts of the Union, I submit a few extracts from sundry publications, issued soon after they made their appearance. It may be proper, however, to premise, that our government (then completely under the influence of the slaveholding interest) was endeavoring to obtain a cession of the territory in question, and that it was at the period of the last invasion of Mexico, by the armies of Spain. The first quotation which I shall make, is from the *Edgefield Carolinian*, a newspaper said to be then under the control of the present Governor M'Duffie, of South Carolina.

" The acquisition of Texas, relinquished by the government of the United States to the *magnanimous* Ferdinand VII. by the *Florida* treaty of 1819, is now a subject of much interest in the western states. This valuable territory has now devolved on the republic of Mexico, and from the condition of that country, *suffering under invasion and civil war*, and *with scanty finances*, it is supposed that the retrocession might be obtained for a reasonable equivalent. Great confidence is expressed that the administration will embrace the present favorable occasion of regaining an extensive and fertile region

* By a reference to a Speech of John Quincy Adams, some extracts from which I will give hereafter, it will be perceived, that our government actually claimed the Texas country, and other parts of the territory adjoining, as far as the Rio Bravo del Norte, when Louisiana was ceded to the United States: and it will also be found, by a reference to the same speech, that this claim could not be sustained, by diplomatic effort, and was *formally abandoned*.
Mr. Adams so forcibly depictures the grasping designs of our slaveholding, land-speculating gentry, that his statements have attracted the attention of thousands in this country and also in Mexico. His speech has been translated into the Spanish language, and published in a pamphlet at the Mexican capital—a copy of which we have received.

of country *within the natural limits of the United States*. Some imposing essays originally published in the St. Louis Beacon, with the signature of ' Americanus,' and attributed to Colonel Benton, of the Senate, explaining the circumstances of the treaty of 1819, and *displaying the advantages* of the retrocession, have operated upon the public mind in the west with electrical force and rapidity. The writer produces strong circumstantial proof that the surrender of Texas resulted from the subserviency of our negotiator to Spain, in her contest with Mexico, together with the powerful subsiding motive of hostility to the southern and western sections of our own country.

" This large fragment of the Mississippi valley, affording sufficient territory for *four or five slaveholding states*, was unceremoniously sacrificed with scarcely a pretext of a demand for it on the part of Spain. The time of the negotiation was during the heat of the debate on the Missouri question—the place was Washington, whither the negotiation had been unnecessarily removed, while it was proceeding prosperously at Madrid, and where the restrictionists were then assembled in all their strength, and the negotiator was Mr. Adams, the friend and associate of the most thorough-going among those restrictionists. ' Americanus ' exposes the evils to the United States of this surrender under twelve distinct heads. Two of them of particular interest to this section of the country, are, that *it brings a non-slaveholding empire in juxtaposition with the slaveholding southwest*, and diminishes the outlet for the Indians inhabiting the States of Georgia, Alabama, Mississippi and Tennessee.''

A Charleston paper also then observed:—

" It is not improbable that he [President Jackson] is now examining the propriety and practicability of a retrocession of the vast territory of Texas, an enterprise loudly demanded by the welfare of the west, and which could not fail to exercise an important and favorable influence upon the future destinies of the South, by increasing the votes of the slaveholding states in the United States *Senate*.''

The Louisiana papers entered warmly into the discussion of the question, about the same time. One of them openly asserted that General Houston had *then* gone to the Texas country, *for the purpose of revolutionizing it*, and observed: " We may expect, shortly, to hear of his raising his flag.''

The *Arkansas Gazette*, a paper thoroughly identified with the slaveholding interest, held forth this language, in the year 1830, respecting the purchase of the Texas country:—

" As the subject of the purchase of Texas has engrossed much of the attention of our politicians for a year or two past, it may not perhaps be improper to state that we are in possession of information, derived from a source entitled to the highest credit, which destroys all hope of the speedy acquisition of that country by the United States. Colonel Butler, the Charge d'Affaires of the United States to Mexico, was specially authorized by the President to treat with that government for the purchase of Texas. The present predominant party are decidedly opposed to the ceding any portion of its territory. [The writer might have added, and so are *all parties*.] No hopes need therefore be entertained of our acquiring Texas, until some other party more friendly to the United States than the present, shall predominate in Mexico, and *perhaps* not until the people of Texas *shall throw off the yoke of allegiance* to that government, which they will do no doubt so soon as they shall have a reasonable *pretext* for doing so.* At present they are probably subject to as few exactions and impositions as any people under the sun."

In addition to 'he writings of various editors of newspapers and their correspondents, we might enumerate the speeches of distinguished political orators, members of legislative bodies, &c. tending to show the general anxiety of the people in our southern states for the acquisition of Texas, and the certain calculations they made on the establishment and perpetuation of slavery therein. I will, however, quote a few from only one or two. In the Virginia Convention of 1829, Judge Usphur, of the Superior Court, observed, in a speech of considerable length, that if Texas should be obtained, which he strongly desired, it would raise the price of slaves, and be a great advantage to the slaveholders in that state.—Mr. Gholson also stated in the Virginia assembly, in the year 1832, that the price of slaves fell *twenty-five per cent.* within two hours after the news was received of the non-importation act which was passed by the Legislature of Louisiana. Yet he believed the acquisition of Texas would raise their price *fifty per cent.* at least.

These *plain indications* of the resolution formed by the slaveholding party in the United States, for the acquisition of the Texas country, opened the eyes of some of our honest citizens. A few of the northern presses spoke out upon the subject. The *Genius of Universal Emancipation*, for September 16th, 1829, then published in Baltimore, contained the following article.—

IMPORTANT RUMOR.

We copy the information below, from the National Journal. The public has been, for some months, acquainted with the fact that Captain Austin has had the grant of certain privileges in navigating the *Rio del Norte* with steam vessels, &c. And it has also been conjectured that a disposition prevailed among some of our politicians to annex the vast tract of country, comprising the Texas and parts, or the whole, of several of the adjoining Mexican provinces, to this Republic. But we have not, until very recently, learned that a project of this kind is not only *on foot*, but that our minister to Mexico is using his influence to induce that government to cede to us the country in question.

This proposition, we think, is of much greater importance than at first meets the eye. Some of our contemporaries speak quite favorably of the adoption of immediate measures for the acquisition of the

* This idea prevailed so generally in Mississippi, at the period here alluded to, that the electors of one district put the following, among other interrogatories, to their candidates for Congress:—

"Your opinion of the acquisition of Texas, and how— whether by force or treaty—and whether the law preventing the emigration of the Americans is not evidence of apprehension that that province wishes to secede from the Mexican government ; and whether, if requested, we ought to give the seceder military assistance; and what would be the effect of the acquisition of Texas upon our planting interest."

territory in question. Others, in noticing it, pass over it without comment.

What, we would ask, would be the consequence of adding so large a territory to our already extensive domain? What the line of policy that will in such an event be pursued with respect to SLAVERY, in said territory? These momentous queries force themselves upon our minds, as subjects of the deepest interest. We shall very soon recur to the general subject, and give our views of it more at length.

TEXAS.—Of the importance of this vast territory, whether viewed geographically or politically, as an appendage to the United States, every one must be well aware. We believe that no man is more sensible ol the value of such an acquisition than our minister to Mexico ; and we believe that a treaty of boundary, by which the Texas should be included in our Republic, has been one of the chief objects of his hopes, and, as far as he could with propriety act, his efforts. The following article, extracted from the Creole, refers to a report that Great Britain has attempted to obtain by purchase this large tract of territory. In the present depressed and distracted condition of Mexico ; a great portion of her capital lost by her impolitic exclusion of the old Spaniards ; and an expedition hostile in its character and designs, on its way to her shores, it is not to be conceived that she will listen with indifference to any offers addressed to her cupidity. It may be a subject well worthy the attention and deliberation of Congress, whether an appropriation to the amount required for the acquisition of this territory, would not be amply compensated by so large an accession to our territorial wealth and political power:

Texas.—Rio Grande del Norte, or Great North River.—Captain Austin has obtained a grant from each of the States through which this river passes, securing to him the exclusive navigation of its waters, and is about to proceed on his first voyage, to ascend it by steam as high as Chihuahua, the capital of the State of that name, a distance of about six hundred miles. A voyage from New Orleans to Metamoras or Refugio, on the del Norte, can be made in three or four days, and thence by steam to Chihuahua in the same time. The Ariel which left New York for this purpose, has an engine of 36 horse power, is about 100 tons burthen, moves at the rate of eleven miles and a half an hour, and draws but three feet four inches water. At high water she can get up to within fifteen leagues of Santa Fe, without being obstructed by the rapids. Thus a journey which now occupies two months, may be performed in a fortnight, and the products of one of the richest and most delightful regions in the world be added to our imports.

A rumor reached us by the last packet from Mexico, (the Virginia,) that a company of British merchants had offered to advance $5,000,000 to the Mexican government on the condition that the province of Texas should be placed under the protection of Great Britain. It was also said that a proposition, would be made by the Mexican government, to put the Texas lands into our possession, on a loan of the above sum. — This would be in contemplation of a treaty of cession to the United States, by which the Rio del Norte will become our southern boundary, if the proposition should still be accepted. The talents and experience of Captain Austin render him every way qualified for the bold project he has conceived, and we hope to see him early crowned with success proportioned to his zeal and activity."

Creole.

In the Nashville Banner of the 21st ult. we find some communications on this subject; in one of which it is recommended to exchange the territory west of the Rocky Mountains for the Province of

Texas. The acquisition of the Texas has been advocated by Mr. Clay, in his speech on the Spanish treaty, in which he also eloquently deprecates the attainment of the province by any foreign power. "If (said he) Texas, after being peopled by us, should at some distant day break off, she will carry with her a noble crew, consisting of our children's children, the sons of freemen."

From one of the communications of the Banner we make the following extract, in reference to this subject.

"The custom-house of New Orleans has paid the purchase money of Louisiana. If there is any man in the Union who has felt himself straitened in his private affairs in consequence of this payment, let him proclaim his name, and he shall have redress—but there is not one.

"The customs of Texas would do the same thing. The Mexican, steeped to the lip in poverty, threatened with a powerful invasion by the mother country, will part with this property or any thing else for the sake of money. Now is the time, and this is the hour, to strike for our country's weal.

"Commercial men, every way qualified to form an estimate and to give an opinion, have said that Texas, in the hands of the British, would be of as much, or more importance to them, than the island of Jamaica. Let us for a moment imagine this delightful region in the hands of that proud and overbearing nation, flinging bones of discord to the two sister republics, and then imagine, if you can, the deep toned imprecations, that would pervade this nation from *Maine* to the *Sabine*, from the sources of the *Missouri* to the mouth of the *Chesapeake*.

"I believe president Jackson has a listening attentive ear. It is said he would as soon scan the opinions of a corporal, as those of a Major General, and that he with equal readiness would adopt or reject either as his judgment might determine. Believing this to be the fact, I venture to make the above suggestion—with the addition that there is not one moment to be lost."

Since the forgoing was put in type, we have seen a numoer of spirited essays upon the subject before us; and we cannot longer disguise the fact, *that the advocates of slavery are resolved, at all hazards to obtain the territory in question, if possible,* FOR THE AVOWED PURPOSE OF ADDING FIVE OR SIX MORE SLAVEHOLDING STATES TO THIS UNION!!!

It is now time for the people of the United States, who are opposed to the further extension of this horrible evil, (an evil unparalleled in the present state of the world,) to AROUSE FROM THEIR LETHARGY, and nip the monstrous attempt in the bud. We therefore call upon them, *with burning anxiety,* to open their eyes to a sense of the approaching danger. A "Missouri Question"—nay, a "Question," vastly more important, is *now* upon the tapis. Let it be duly considered; and let the public voice, *from every quarter of the Republic,* denounce in tones of thunder, the *unhallowed proceeding.*

It must be borne in mind, that the system of slavery *has been abolished in Texas,* by the Mexican government. It is now a FREE STATE. But the *avowed* design of Senator *Benton,* and others of his political clan, is to change this state of things, and introduce the slave system, with all its barbarities, again. Should the territory be added to this Union, *upon the condition that slavery should still be* INTERDICTED, a great number of the colored people in the United States, at least those bordering

on the Mississippi, might be induced to remove thither. *It would be the most suitable place for them in the world.* But a GREATER CURSE could scarcely befall our country, than the annexation of that immense territory to this Republic, if the system of slavery should likewise be re-established there.

The present Administration of the general government is believed to be in favor of obtaining this territory, *with the view of increasing the number of Slaveholding States.* It is, indeed, boldly intimated in the *National Intelligencer,* that NEGOTIATIONS FOR IT ARE NOW PENDING. Again we say: Let the public sentiment be expressed.—Let the moral influence of the people—(the honest yeomanry of the nation)—be heard, from the highest peak of our mountains to the lowest valley—from the northern and eastern confines of the Union to its farthest southern and western limits. A more important occasion for such an expression of their will never occurred, and perhaps never may again. We shall not let the matter rest here."

The *Genius of Universal Emancipation,* for September 25th, (the week following) pursues the subject as follows:

"THE PURCHASE OF TEXAS.

This subject now resolves itself into a *National Question* of the utmost importance—the LIMITATION AND CIRCUMSCRIPTION, or the EXTENSION and PERPETUATION, of AMERICAN SLAVERY. It will be in vain for any one to place a different construction upon the proposition. The quarter in which it originates; the champions who step forth in its defence; the time selected for its accomplishment;—but above all, the *argument used* to shew its propriety, prove as clearly as even the most indubitable evidence can prove, that the great and leading object of its advocates is to enlarge the boundaries of the region of Slavery, and extend the period of its duration, in this Republic.

It is well understood in the political circles, that the most active promoter of this scheme is no less a personage than the famous THOMAS H. BENTON, now a Senator in the Congress of the United States, and to whom the State of *Missouri* is more indebted than any other man, for the "blessings" of slavery, which have been entailed upon her. Benton is a man possessed of some good qualities. While his political principles, so far as they relate to slavery, are of the most detestable cast, *hypocrisy* is not, by any means, a conspicuous trait in his character. In general, he speaks out, boldly, the tyrannical aristocracy of his heart; and an opponent may always know where to find him. We knew him well, as a chivalrous quill-driver, during the period of the Missouri contest. Then, as now, he strenuously advocated the unlimited exercise of all the odious "privileges and immunities" of a hereditary, irresponsible slaveholder:—and, indeed, he *practically* understood the nature of the cause he espoused.

The essays now publishing in the newspapers, over the signature of "*Americanus,*" urging the immediate purchase of the province of Texas, are said to be from the pen of this ambitious, political aspirant. Of the correctness of the supposition we have not a shadow of doubt. Now, as formerly, he unblushingly advocates the whole system of slavery, without any qualification whatever. One of the reasons that he assigns (and one which he seems to consider the strongest) for the purchase of Texas, is, as we have before stated, that *five or six more slaveholding states" may thus be added to the*

Union.—Indeed, he goes farther than this in one of his calculations, and estimates that "NINE MORE STATES, *as large as Kentucky*," may be formed within the limits of that province. He undertakes also, by much more than dubious insinuation, to shew that this would *give the slaveholding states a preponderating influence in the councils of the nation.* He likewise asserts, that the United States once had a rightful claim to the province of Texas, by virtue of the Louisiana purchase; but that (he continues) it was lost *through the influence of the non-slaveholding interest in Congress.* This being his view of the matter he now calculates that the SLAVE-ITE PARTY is strong enough to reverse the existing state of things, and *open a new world,* as it were, for the employment of slave-labor, like the colonial projectors have generally done before him, since the discovery of the American continent by the Europeans. There is a little difference, however, in the mode heretofore adopted for supplying the demand for slaves and that which he now has in contemplation. Instead of a dependence upon the African slave-trade, he would convert the whole extent of country, where slave-labor is unprofitable, and where provisions are cheap, into *an immense nursery for slaves,* and by this means people those more southern regions with a race of serviles (part of whom would be bred especially for the purpose) *at least twice as fast as it could be done by the foreign importation alone.* This would indeed be a splendid project! worthy of the capacious mind of a BENTON, who, we must admit, is fully competent to school a Hawkins, or a D'Wolf, in matters of this nature. The boldness with which he advocates measures so repugnant to the feelings of the more religious and moral portion of the community, would seem to savour somewhat of rashness. No other statesman, perhaps, would dare, at this period of republican reformation, and in this era of republican light, to utter the tyrannical sentiments that he does, on slavery, at least in so open and undisguised a manner. He must have great confidence in the strength of the *slaveite party;* or, otherwise, he must calculate largely upon the aid of the *"dough faced"* gentry of the non-slaveholding states. To secure the co-operation of these, every appeal will be made to their cupidity—every inducement held out that the hope of governmental patronage under the present dynasty, can conjure up.—And that some of them will prove recreant in the hour of trial, and lash themselves to the car of despotism, past experience leaves us no room to doubt, How many will thus degrade themselves, and disgrace the land of their birth, time alone will show.

We are glad to find, since the last number of our paper was issued, that the subject before us is viewed in the same light as we view it, by some of our most respectable contemporaries. The *Pennsylvania Gazette,* of Philadelphia, and the *American,* of New York, have come out in plain terms, and express in a decided tone their apprehensions, as follows:—

From the Pennsylvania Gazette,

' The acquisition of the Texas promises to be a leading measure of the present administration, and without doubt, one of great magnitude and importance. This will be very apparent from the fact as stated, that the territory in question will make nine states, as large as Kentucky; to which add the apalling consideration that it is designed to make these nine states *slave states.* We are told also, that " the proper steps have been taken to procure the cession." It is high time, for the northern interest,

the non-slaveholding states, to look around, to see how the balance of power, which it was the object of the federal constitution to create and preserve, will be effected by this bold undertaking. We are much pleased with the following remarks of the New York American.

' The Richmond Enquirer, with one of its hints that are meant to signify a great deal, says—' The Statesmen who are at the head of our affairs, are not the men we take them to be, if they have not already pursued the proper steps for obtaining the cession of Texas. even before the able Nos. of Americanus saw the light. But, *nous verrons!'* We are therefore to understand, that measures are already in train for the recovery of Texas. ' The able numbers of Americanus' put the importance of this recovery to Southern men and Southern interest, on the ground of the space and advatages that country will afford, for, 'the future existence of Slave States.' Within the boundaries of Texas, ' nine States,' says Americanus. ' as large as Kentucky may be formed.' With the immense benefits before our eyes secured to the United States by the acquisition of Louisiana, we should be cautious in pronouncing against the expediency of endeavoring to obtain. for a fair equivalent, so fine a province as Texas, and which runs in, in various parts. upon what may, perhaps, be not improperly called our national boundaries. Yet, on the other hand, when the great, and, as we do not hesitate to say, unjust preponderance of the Slave States, in the existing confederacy, is considered, it may well cause the inhabitants of the free states to pause, and maturely to consider the effect upon our institutions and Union, of the increase, by the half dozen, of these states— bound together by one common bond of peril, of profit, and of political power. The moral considerations, too, which belong to this subject, connected with the new and vast market that this province would open to the domestic slave-trade--not less atrocious in principle, if somewhat milder in practice, than that which on the coast of Africa is pronounced piracy, and punished with death---will not fail to present themselves with force to the minds of all considerate men.'

The stand thus taken by the respectable and influential papers above named, inspires the hope that the more reflecting part of our fellow citizens will thwart the intentions of the advocates of slavery, in the present case, and put this gigantic scheme to rest for a season. We were aware that a deadly apathy existed, relative to the subject under review, and felt it our duty to sound the tocsin of alarm. Whatever we may think of the purchase of the territory in question, with the view of colonizing our colored people there *by themselves,* we do not think it would be safe to do it at the present period. True, the majority of the people are opposed to the extension of slavery; but will that majority act efficiently at the present time? We have strong doubts of this; and are decidedly of the opinion that the wisest policy will be to defer the purchase, until the public mind is fully prepared to restrict the extension of slavery beyond the limits of its present existence.'

The evidence thus exhibited of a disposition in the people and government of this country to obtain the territory in question, even contrary to the expressed wishes of the Mexicans, induced their statesmen to take a very serious view of the subject. The following is an extract from a paper laid before the Mexican Congress, in the year 1829, by the Secretary of State. A strong appeal was made to the nation, to sustain the government in resisting what was alleged to be a premeditated and determined encroachment upon their territorial sovereignty. I shall copy, however, but a small portion of his remarks.

"The North Americans commence by introducing themselves into the territory which they covet on pretence of commercial negotiations or of the establishment of colonies, with or without the assent of the Government to which it belongs. These colonies grow, multiply, become the predominant part in the population; and as soon as a support is found in this manner, they begin to set up rights which it is impossible to sustain in a serious discussion, and to bring forward ridiculous pretensions, founded upon historical facts which are admitted by nobody, such as Lasalle's Voyages, now known to be a falsehood, but which serves as a support, at this time, for their claim to Texas. These extravagant opinions, are for the first time, presented to the world by unknown writers; and the labor which is employed by others in offering proofs and reasonings, is spent by them in repetitions and multiplied allegation, for the purpose of drawing the attention of their fellow citizens, not upon the justice of the proposition, but upon the advantages and interests to be obtained or subverted by their admission.

"Their machinations in the country they wish to acquire, are then brought to light by the appearance of explorers, some of whom settle on the soil, alleging that their presence does not affect the question of the right of sovereignty or possession of the land. These pioneers excite by degrees, movements which disturb the political state of the country in dispute; and then follow discontents and dissatisfaction calculated to fatigue the patience of the legitimate owner, and to diminish the usefulness of the administration and of the exercise of authority. When things have come to this pass, which is precisely the present state of things in Texas, the diplomatic management commences. The inquietude they have excited in the territory in dispute, the interests of the colonists therein established, the insurrection of adventurers and savages instigated by them, and the pertinacity with which the opinion is set up as to their right of possession, become the subjects of notes full of expressions of justice and moderation, until, with the aid of other incidents which are never wanting in the course of diplomatic relations, the desired end is attained of concluding an arrangement onerous for one party as it is advantageous to the other.

"It has been said further, that when the United States of the North have succeeded in giving the predominance to the colonists introduced into the countries they had in view, they set up rights, and bring forward pretensions founded upon disputed historical facts, availing themselves generally, for the purpose of some critical conjuncture to which they suppose that the attention of Government must be directed. This policy, which has produced good results to them, they have commenced carrying into effect with Texas. The public prints in those states, including those which are more immediately under the influence of their government, are engaged in discussing the right they imagine they have to the country as far as the Rio Bravo. Hand-bills are printed on the same subject, and thrown into general circulation, whose object is to persuade and convince the people of the utility and expediency of the meditated project. Some of them have said that Providence had marked out the Rio Bravo as the natural boundary of those states, which has induced an English writer to reproach them with an attempt to make Providence the author of their usurpations; but what is most remarkable, is, that

they have commenced that discussion precisely at the same time they saw us engaged in repelling the Spanish invasion, believing that our attention would, for a long time be thereby withdrawn from other things."*

Whether the charges here made were correct, or not, I leave to the decision of the intelligent reader and impartial historian. Such, however, were the impressions that were made upon the minds of well informed Mexicans, and such the manner in which they expressed their sentiments. Some of the writers for their public presses were very pointed and severe. One of them, in speaking of the efforts of our diplomatic agent, to alienate the territory from the Mexican Republic, speaks thus:—" That when he found his offer objectionable, he further insulted the nation by proposing a loan of ten millions, as a pawn-broker would, upon the pawning of Texas until repaid, which insidious proposal was meant to fill the country of Texas with Anglo-Americans and slaves, and to hold it afterwards in any event: that citizens of the United States encourage the excursions of the Comanches, and other predatory tribes, against the Mexican frontier settlements, furnishing them with arms, and buying their stolen mules, and even Mexican freemen, such as mulattoes and Indians, to be held as slaves in Louisiana, &c.: that they have suggested to the Texas colonists at various times to rebel, and declare the country independent of Mexico, or even ask an union with the United States of the North, who will allow the bane of slavery."

The excitement produced among the Mexicans, by the efforts above alluded to, was very great; and upon the strength of these impressions, the general Congress passed the law of April 6th, 1830, prohibiting the further migration of Anglo-Americans into Texas. The jealousy of the British government was also aroused, and the subject was noticed in the lower House of Parliament. A debate occurred, in which the celebrated Mr. HUSKISSON took a leading part, that manifested the liveliest interest in the independence of the Mexican Republic, and the integrity of its territory. It would require too much space at present to insert the speeches, made during this discussion; but a brief synopsis, or hasty review of it, is here given from the London "Times":—

"Mr. Huskisson, in presenting the Liverpool petition on the subject of their relations with Spain and Mexico, in the course of last night, urged with great force the propriety of preventing Spain from making further attacks from the side of Cuba, on the now liberated Republic of Mexico.

"There was a further subject, and one of extreme importance, discussed by Mr. Huskisson, in the course of his speech—we mean the general prevalence of an opinion that the United States covet a fine province of Mexico, called Texas, and are disposed to have recourse to violence, if necessary, for the purpose of getting it into their hands. The province of Texas extends southwards from the United States along the coast of Mexico, and as such, the seizure of it by the former power could not be a matter of perfect indifference to Great Britain. The possession of the Floridas by the United States has long since given rational cause of uneasiness to England, from regard to the safety of our West India Islands; and we agree with Mr. Huskisson, that when the government of Washington intimated its repugnance to seeing Cuba transferred from the feeble Ferdinand

---

* See the extract from the "Nashville Banner," in a preceding column. I believe that the article was written precisely at this juncture—and the writer concludes by saying, " there is not one moment to be lost."

to the vigorous grasp of George IV., the United States should have been informed that if Cuba were to continue permanently Spanish, so Texas, and in general the whole shore along the Gulf, should ensure to the Mexican republic.

" The reference made by the Right Hon. Gentleman to communications, official as well as private, from the late Mr. Jefferson, descriptive of the eager and deep rooted longings of the American statesmen for slices of Mexico, and above all things, for the Island of Cuba, will not, we are sure, be lost upon the memory of his Majesty's Government in its future transactions with the Spanish Cabinet, with that of Mexico, and of the United States. With Spain we have a defensive alliance, ready made and consolidated,by the most obvious interest, to prevent Cuba from falling a prey to the systematic aggrandizement of the United States. With Mexico, we are equally identified in resistance to the attempts of the same States upon Texas "

It must be observed that the principal advocates of measures for the acquisition of Texas, in the United States, previous to this period, were the southern slaveholders;—and their influence was now paramount in the Cabinet. But finding that the territory could not be obtained by negotiation and purchase, and well knowing that no legal claim to it could possibly be sustained, the government declined pressing the matter further at the time. The writers for the newspaper press, too, now ceased to urge it upon the public attention. Yet the scheme was by no means abandoned. A different mode of operations was planned and adopted, for the ultimate and certain accomplishment of their object. It was known that nearly all the colonists in Texas were originally from our slaveholding States, and either slave-holders themselves, or friendly to the re-establishment and perpetuation of the system of slavery there. The plan thenceforth pursued was, to misrepresent the Mexican laws and colonial regulations, relative to slavery, and induce the emigration of persons favourable to their views, until their numerical and physical strength should enable them to take advantage of some critical conjuncture, and subject the country, at least, to their legislative control. Should they succeed in this they believed that they would, finally, be able to carry their whole design into effect—which could be done either by the future attachment of the territory to the northern Union, or to a new confederacy that might eventually be organized, still more favorable to the principle and practice of slaveholding. As I have stated before, in my previous remarks, the private correspondence kept up for this purpose was very extensive, and the emigration from our southern states to the Texas country continued to increase. Slaves were taken in without hesitation, and men of wealth, enterprise, and influence, throughout the southern and south-western States, lent their countenance and aid to the scheme.

From the commencement of their operations, we have seen, that the "choice spirits" of that extensive, unholy combination of slaveholders and land-jobbers, who have swayed the destinies of Texas, have steadily and undeviatingly pursued their object. They have constantly adhered to their settled, original purpose, however they may have occasionally relaxed their open, undisguised efforts. It is true, their rashness sometimes led them into the adoption of premature measures, and they were compelled to halt, and even to retrace their steps, for the moment. Those who had neither character nor property at stake, and those at a distance from the scene of action, were more reckless of consequences than the substantial settlers in the country, on whom the weight of responsibility must necessarily fall. This was strikingly exemplified in the case of Austin's treasonable attempt, which resulted in his imprisonment by order of the general government. Calculating on the intestine difficulties of the Republic, he was prompted to the commission of overt acts before their plans were sufficiently matured. The following letter (to which I have before alluded) will throw some additional light upon this part of our subject. It will be seen that he was pushed forward against his own will and better judgment, while he candidly admits that the colonists had no cause of complaint against the government. Some precious confessions, indeed, are here recorded, which cannot fail to make the most forcible impressions on the mind of the reader.

From the New Orleans Bulletin.

The following letter from Col. Stephen F. Austin, was written immediately after his arrest by the Mexican Government, and is published in our latest Texas papers. We re-publish it as interesting to those who are seeking information of that fertile and promising region, its government and politics.

MONTERREY, Jan. 17, 1834.

To the Ayuntamiento of San Felipe de Austin:

I have been arrested by an order from the minister of war, and leave soon for Mexico to answer to a charge made against me, as I understand, for writing an officio to the Ayuntamiento of Bexar, dated 21st October last, advising, or rather recommending that they should consult amongst themselves for the purpose of organizing a local government for Texas, in the event that no remedies could be obtained for the evils that threatened that country with ruin.

I do not in any manner blame the Government for arresting me, and I particularly request that there may be no excitement about it.

I give the advice to the people there, that I have always given, keep quiet, discountenance all revolutionary measures or men, obey the State authorities and laws so long as you are attached to Coahuila, have no more conventions, *petition through the legal channels,* that is through the Ayuntamiento and chief of department, harmonize fully with the people of Bexar and Goliad, and act with them.

The general government are disposed to do every thing for Texas that can be done to promote its prosperity and welfare that is consistent with the constitution and laws, and I have no doubt the state government will do the same if they are applied to in a proper manner.

It will be remembered that I went to Mexico as a public agent with specific instructions, and as such, that it was my duty to be governed by them, and by the general wish of the people as expressed to me.* Also, that when I left in April, the general wish did express itself for the separation from Coahuila and the forming of Texas into a State of this confederation. Also, that there was a determination to organize a local government at all hazards, if no remedy could be obtained.

I have in all my acts conformed to this public wish of the people, so far as I was informed of it; and when I despaired of obtaining any remedy, as I did in the beginning of October, I deemed it to be my duty as an agent, to inform the people so; and believing as I did, that they would organize, I also considered that it would be much better to do so, by a harmonious consultation of the Ayuntamientos, than by a popular commotion. There were many reasons for the recommendation given in that officio; also, the result of the civil war was thought to be doubtful.

I understand and I rejoice to hear it, that public opinion has settled down on *a more reasonable basis,* and that the most of the Ayuntamientos of Texas have expressed their wish to proceed in a *legal manner* to seek redress. I ought to have been informed of this change, but I was not, and knew nothing of it to a certainty, until the 5th of November, so that up to that time I acted under the impressions I had when I left Texas in April. Since then I have not moved the state question.

The past events in Texas necessarily grew out of the revolution of Jalapa, which overturned the constitution and produced the counter revolution of Vera Cruz, which extended over the whole country, and involved Texas with the rest. It is well known that it was my wish to keep Texas, and particularly the colony, out of all revolution, and I tried to do so, but the flame broke out in my absence from Texas, in June 1832, and since then all has been completely disjointed. A current was set in motion by the general extent of the civil war all over the nation, and under the circumstances, Texas could not avoid being agitated by it. No one can be blamed in any manner for what has happened since June 1832, in Texas—it was inevitable—neither was it possible for me to avoid being drawn into the whirlpool. It was my duty to serve the country as an agent if requested to do so; and as an agent it was my duty to obey my instructions as expressed to me.

I have long since informed the Ayuntamiento of Texas, of the repeal of the law of April, and of the *favorable and friendly disposition of the government,* and by this, I of course rescinded, or annulled the recommendation of 2d October, for that was predicated on the belief that nothing would be done, and that the result of the civil war then pending was doubtful; since then all has changed for the better, and public opinion in Texas has become sound,† and shaken off the excitement that necessarily grew out of the past agitations.

Under these circumstances the prospects of Texas are better than they ever have been. The national revolution is ended, and a constitutional government

exists, the people are obedient to the government and laws every where. Be the same in Texas, and have no more excitements, *tolerate no more violent measures, and you will prosper and obtain from the government, all that reasonable men ought to ask for.*

The last year has been one of calamities for Texas—floods, pestilence, and commotions, I hope the present year will be more favorable. I request that you will have this letter published for general information, and also the enclosed copy of the answer given to me by his Excellency the minister of relations. You will see by this answer the very favorable and friendly disposition of the general government to make a state or a territory of Texas, and do every thing else within its constitutional powers for the good of that country.

I consider my agency for Texas as terminated, but this will not prevent me from doing all I can for the good of that country, on my own individual responsibility.

Respectfully your most ob't serv't.

STEPHEN F. AUSTIN.

On the 10th of May, 1834, he also wrote as follows, from the place of his confinement at the seat of government. He does not admit that he had entertained the design of transferring the country to the government of the United States. No one will suspect that *he* had indulged a wish of that kind. It was his desire to be *at the head of political affairs* in Texas; and were it attached to the United States he would soon witness a *rivalry* that must eventually blast his hopes. But many others concerned in Texas politics, *did* contemplate the transfer in question; and, even according to Austin's confessions, the better disposed part of the *inhabitants,* himself included, were dictated to, and *ruled,* by the land-speculating and slave-trafficking banditti, who had more convenient opportunities to concentrate their efforts. The letter from which the following is extracted, was directed to a gentleman in New Orleans.—

" I have been in close and solitary confinement here until yesterday, since the 13th February. Yesterday I was allowed to communicate with persons outside, receive books, writing materials, visits, &c. I expect to be at liberty in a short time, and shall probably return by way of Orleans. My confinement has been very rigid, but I have received no personal ill treatment. The good people of the Colony precipitated me into these difficulties, by their excitements. I came here as the agent of excited and fevered constituents, and I represented them regardless of my personal safety or welfare. I was much more impatient and of coarse imprudent than cold calculating prudence would sanction, but not more so than the tone and temper of my constituents required when I left them. I do not blame the Vice President or Government for arresting me—an attempt has been made to charge me with designs to separate Texas from Mexico and deliver it to the U. States of the North—that is totally false and without the shadow of foundation, as all are now convinced; so that I have no doubt I shall soon leave this place."

In order to make the reader more familiar with the proceedings of those concerned in this splendid project, in various parts of America, I will now present a succinct, though comprehensive view of their combined operations. Many individuals in other countries

* This " general wish" was not *expressed* by the great mass of the actual settlers in the colonies. No measures were adopted to ascertain the "general" wishes of the people. The sentiments thus *expressed,* were the clamors of the land-speculators and aspirants to power and office, and the urgent demands of lordly slaveholders, both resident and transient, among them. The more sober and orderly *inhabitants* were very generally opposed to it.

† " Public opinion in Texas has *become* sound !"—The *actual settlers* had then more *generally* expressed their " wishes ;" and the rebellious slaveites and marauders had found that they had pushed ahead *too soon.*—The writer himself was in a delicate and *difficult* situation, and a little prudent *policy* must be used to extricate him. His conduct eventually proved *how sincere* were his own professions of attachment to Mexico.

have a hand in it;—yet its *active promoters* are principally citizens of the United States.

The Republic of Mexico, from the period of its organization, evinced the utmost liberality towards foreigners in granting permission to colonize its vacant lands, until that liberality, and the confidence reposed in their friendly disposition, were grossly abused, particularly by those who proceeded from our own country. Of the immense tracts of land designated for colonization, in the various contracts entered into with the different "Empresarios," those granted to Zavala, Vehlein, and Burnet, were united and transferred to a company in New York, called the "Galvezton Bay and Texas Land Company." This Association was fully organized on the 16th of October, 1830. The following named persons were appointed as Directors, viz: Lynde Catlin, William G. Bucknor, George Griswold, Barney Corse, John Hagerty, Dudley Seldon, and Stephen Whitney. The following were also chosen as trustees, viz: Anthony Dey, George Curtis, W. H. Sumner. It is believed, however, that some of these subsequently declined acting, and others were appointed in their places. The contract entered into by the Government with Zavala, was concluded on the 12th of March 1829; with Vehlein, 21st December, 1826, and a second on the 11th October, 1828; with Burnet, 22d December, 1826. The grants to Dominguez, and Wilson & Exter, were in like manner conveyed to Elisha Tibbits, John S. Crary, Henry Hone and their associates, under the title of the "*Arkansas and Texas Land Company*," by whom Thomas Ludlow Ogden, Daniel Jackson, and Edward Curtis, were appointed Trustees to hold the same, &c.—Another company was organized at Nashville, Tennessee, and the grants made to Ross and Leftwitch were transferred to it, upon the same principle. A third company was likewise formed in New York, at a subsequent date, entitled the "*Rio Grand Company*," (I believe,) which agreed to colonize the tracts obtained by Grant & Beales, and Soto & Egerton, as well as others. These several companies created "stocks" upon the basis of those "grants," and threw them into the market. They also issued "scrip," authorizing the holders of it to take possession of certain tracts of land, within the lines marked out on the map as the boundaries of their respective grants. This "scrip" embraced tracts of various dimensions, and was sold to any who could be induced to purchase, at such prices as could be obtained. To a bona fide settler, (and none else could obtain the land it pretended to convey,) it could be of no advantage whatever, as the facilities and expense of procuring his tract, according to law, would be the same whether he held the scrip or not. Every cent paid for it, therefore, was so much loss to the settler, and gain to the company. Although these companies could only hold

their grants through the Medium of the Empresarios, for the limited period of six years, and on the express condition of settling a specified number of families, they dealt largely in their "stock," and sold immense quantities of "scrip," insomuch that an immense amount of money has no doubt been realized by them—while very few settlers (in many of the grants *none*) have been introduced. By obtaining from the government an extension of the time stipulated for the fulfilment of contracts made with the Empresarios, they have been enabled to continue and increase their operations upon a grand scale. Thousands in various parts of the United States have purchased the scrip issued by them, and are interested, of course, in the adoption of measures to legalize their claims. This can never be done, however, while the laws are in force, under which the colonization privileges were obtained. When these companies were first organized, some honorable men engaged in their speculations, that were, doubtless, actuated by honest motives: but many have since joined in the scheme, who are reckless of all principle except that of money-making. The "scrip" being transferable, a large portion of it has fallen into the hands of needy adventurers, who likewise are willing to encourage any measures that may seem calculated to promote their immediate pecuniary interests.

To show more clearly how utterly at variance were these measures with the regulations adopted by the government for the settlement of the country, I here copy the Law enacted by the State Legislature, prescribing the terms upon which foreigners were permitted to colonize the vacant lands in Texas.—I believe this law has never before been published, at length, in the United States—at least I have not hitherto seen a *translation* of it in print. A reference to it will be useful, as well to elucidate the liberal views and propositions of the government, as to exhibit the dishonest practices of slaveholders and land-jobbers, who have parcelled out the territory among themselves and their associate adventurers. Although the law, here quoted, is not the first that was enacted to encourage the colonization of the Texas Country, it is nearly the same as the one originally promulgated—being merely a revision of the statute, with a few trifling alterations in details, without changing its general features or principles.

COLONIZATION LAW OF COAHUILA & TEXAS.

Supreme Government of the State of Coahuila & Texas.
The Governor of the State of Coahuila & Texas to all the inhabitants—health. The Congress of the said State has passed the following Decree.
[DECREE No. 190.]
The Constitutional Congress of the free, independent, and sovereign State of Coahuila & Texas, decrees as follows:

ARTICLE 1.—Those Mexicans who, at the period of the publication of this law, shall determine to settle any of the vacant land belonging to the State, are hereby offered asylum and protection.

ART. 2.—Any Mexican, or Mexicans, who shall propose to introduce, at his or their own expense, Ninety Families, at least, shall present themselves to the Government, and enter into contract, in conformity with this law ; and the territory, in which they are to establish themselves, shall be pointed out—which contract shall be fulfilled within four years. Those who do not establish the said number of families, shall forfeit the rights and privileges hereby granted.

ART. 3.—So soon as Thirty Families shall be collected, they shall proceed to the formal establishment of new Towns, in the most convenient places in the opinion of the Government, or of the person commissioned by it, for that purpose ; and for each new Town, four square Leagues of land shall be designated, the figure of which may be regular, or irregular, according to its location.

ART. 4.—If any site where a new Town shall be formed belong to an individual, and the establishment may be of known and general utility, it shall still be formed—observing the regulations of the Constitution, in the fourth restriction of Article 113.

ART. 5.—The Government, in consideration of the agreement which any contractor, or contractors, shall enter into, and for the better location and formation of the new towns, and the exact division of soil and water, shall commission a confidential person, who shall be of Mexican origin, and not enjoy foreign privileges, who shall proceed according to the instructions of the 4th of September, 1827, when not in opposition to this law.

ART. 6.—In Towns which admit of water works, they will be constructed for account of those concerned. The Commissioner will divide the water off in pipes, or conduits, endeavoring to make them at least half a yard wide; one of which shall be for the use of the Town, and the others for irrigating the fields.

ART. 7.—The contractor and new settlers, in the division and location of land and water, shall be at no other expense than the pay of the commissioner and surveyor, according to law.

ART. 8.—To each Family, included in the contract, referred to in Art. 2, shall be given one Day of water, and one Labor of land, [177 acres] or two if the land is temporal, [cannot be irrigated] and a Town lot of 70 yards square, on which they shall build a house, within two years, under pain of forfeiture of their privilege. Should they possess over one hundred head of stock—either of cattle or horses —or six hundred head of small stock, they shall be entitled to a Sitio [4428 acres] of pasture land.

ART. 9.—A square of land, which on each side measures one League, of 5000 Varas—or, what is the same, an area or superficies of 25,000,000 square varas—shall be called a Sitio ; and this shall be the unit for counting one, two, or more Sitios ; as likewise, the unit for counting one, two, or more Labors, shall be one million square varas, or one thousand varas on each side, which shall constitute a Labor. The vara, for these admeasurements, shall consist of three geometrical feet.

ART. 10.—This Law concedes to the contractors, for each Ninety Families which shall be established in the new settlements, four Sitios of grazing land, and three days of water in each supply that can be used for cultivation of the settlement. But they can take only that proportion for nine hundred families, though a greater number should be established—nor shall they have the right to any premium for any fraction, not reaching to ninety.

ART. 11.—No Commissioner, nor any other authority, can give to the same person a second Lot, unless he shall have built upon the first.

ART. 12.—The contractor who, on account of the Families he shall establish, shall acquire, according to Art. 10. more than Eleven Sitios, must dispose of the excess within nine years. And if he does not do so, the respective civil authorities shall put it up at public auction, and pay over to the owners the net proceeds, deducting the expenses of the sale.

ART. 13.—The Government can sell to Mexicans, such lands as they wish,---with the proviso, that no single person obtain more than eleven Sitios, and under the express condition, that the purchaser have introduced into said lands, by the fourth year of his purchase, at the least Thirty head of large, and Two hundred head of small cattle, for each Sitio. The purchaser shall pay into the Treasury of the state, or wherever the Government shall direct, at the time of sale, the fourth part of the land sold ; and the three remaining parts shall be paid the second, third, and fourth years, respectively, under penalty of forfeiting his right to any part, and losing the whole by his failure to comply with this arrangement.

ART. 14.—The price of each Sitio, within ten leagues in a straight line from the shores of the gulf of Mexico, shall be Two Hundred Dollars, if it be of grazing land, and Three Hundred if of temporal. In the rest of the Department of Bejar, the value shall be One Hundred Dollars, if it be of grazing land, and One Hundred and Fifty, if of temporal. And in the other commons of the State, the value shall be Fifteen Dollars, for grazing land, and Twenty for temporal.

ART. 15.—The Government will sell to Mexicans, alone, the land which by its local situation, will admit of irrigation, and shall not be marked out for settlements, at Three Hundred Dollars each Sitio, in the Department of Bejar,---and in other parts of the State at Two Hundred Dollars,---according to terms in Art. 13, on the express condition, that by the fourth year from the purchase, the purchaser shall have the eighth part of the land under cultivation---observing the same rule with respect to the temporal lands as mentioned in the foregoing article.

ART. 16.—There shall be no variation in regard to the contracts which the Government shall have entered into, nor in the grants which it shall have made to purchasers or settlers, in virtue of the Decree, No. 16, of 24th March, 1825 ; but care shall be taken that those who shall have purchased, within eighteen months after the publication of this law, enter into possession of the lands granted to them.

Upon those of the former class, who shall hereafter make new contracts, or shall hold new grants in the way of purchase, (i. e. in virtue of the Decree No. 16, of the 24th March, 1825,) it shall be obligatory to make, within eighteen months from the execution of their respective contracts, settlements on their lands of one-sixth part of the families stipulated in their said contracts ; and those of the second class (to wit, those who shall have purchased within eighteen months after the publication of this law) shall, within the period specified in their contracts, actually enter into possession of the lands under the penalty of forfeiting them by not observing this regulation.

ART. 17.—Every new settlement shall be free from all contributions whatever, for the space of ten years from the time of its establishment, except such as shall be laid, generally, to prevent or repel foreign invasion.

ART. 18.—The Families which shall, at their own expense, remove to any of the new settlements, and wish to establish themselves in any of them, can do so at any time ; and shall therefore be entitled to the benefits granted by this law to new settlers ; for which purpose they shall present themselves to the Commissioner, or, in his absence, to the respective civil authority, in order that, by making themselves known to the Government, they may receive their grants in due form.

Art. 19.—No new settler, whether Mexican or Foreigner, shall sell, or alienate in any manner, or under any pretext, the water or land in his possession, until after having entered upon and possessed the same during six years.

Art. 20.—A Mexican or a Foreigner, who shall undertake to colonize with foreign families, whose introduction is not prohibited by the general law, of 6th April, 1830, shall be entitled to the benefits conceded in Art. 10, of this law.

Art. 21.—The division of the land and water to foreign families, as set forth in Articles 18 and 20, shall be made in conformity to Art. 8, provided the conditions required by this law are complied with—they paying to the State one third less price than is set forth in Art. 14, in the following terms : One-half of the value in two years from taking possession, and the balance in six years.

Art. 22.—To such Families, as are referred to in the preceding article, shall be given half a Sitio of grazing land, provided they possess the number of large and small cattle, required in the second part of Article 8.

Art. 23.—The Ayuntamientos of each municipality shall collect the above mentioned funds, gratis, by means of a Committee, appointed either within or without their body ; and shall remit them, as they are collected, to the Treasurer of their funds, who will give the corresponding receipt, and without any other compensation than two and an half per cent which is all that shall be allowed him ; he shall hold them at the disposition of the Government, rendering an account, every month, of the ingress or egress, and of any remissness or fraud which he may observe in their collection ; for the correct management of all which, the person employed, and the committee, and the individuals of the ayuntamientos who appoint them, shall be individually responsible; and that this responsibility may be at all times effectual, the said appointments shall be made viva voce, and information shall be given thereof immediately to the Government.

Art. 24.—Foreigners, in order to be admitted as new settlers, must competently prove, before the Commissioner, and on his responsibility, their good morals, belief in Christianity, and good conduct. These indispensible requisites are to be set forth in the Book, Becerro, mentioned in Article 9, of the instructions of 4th September, 1827.

Art. 25.—The Government will take care that, in the Twenty Leagues, bordering on the United States of America, and Ten Leagues in a straight line from the coast of the gulf of Mexico, in the bounds of the State, no establishment shall be made which shall not consist of two-thirds of Mexicans, obtaining, by anticipation, the approbation of the Supreme Government of the Union; to which effect information shall be sent of all proceedings which shall be made in the matter, whether the undertakers be Mexicans or Foreigners.

Art. 26.—In the distribution of lands, native Mexicans shall be preferred to foreigners ; and no other distinction shall be made between the former, except what is based upon their particular merit and their services done to the country—or, other circumstances being equal, their nearness to the place where the lands are situated.

Art. 27.—The Indians, of all nations, bordering upon the State, as well as the wandering tribes within it, shall be received in the markets without exacting from them any commercial duties upon their trade in articles of the country. And, if thus drawn,

by the gentleness and confidence with which they shall also be treated, they shall, declaring themselves first in favor of our religion and institutions, establish themselves in any part of the settlements which shall be formed, they shall be admitted, and allowed the same terms as other settlers, treated of in this law, distinguishing the natives as Mexicans, and the borderers as foreigners, without exacting from the first any number of cattle.

Art. 28.—In order that there may be no vacancies, between tracts, of which great care shall be taken in the distribution of lands, they shall be laid off in squares, or other forms although irregular, if the local situation requires it; and in said distribution, as well as in the assignation of lands for new Towns, previous notice shall be given to the adjoining proprietors, (if any) in order to prevent dissentions and law-suits.

Art. 29.—The quantity of vacant land which has to be laid out upon the banks of a river, rivulet, stream, or lake, shall not, if practicable, exceed a fourth part of the whole depth of the tract granted.

Art. 30.—If, by error in the grant, any land shall be conceded, belonging to another individual, on proof being made of that fact, an equal quantity shall be granted, elsewhere, to the person who may have thus obtained it through mistake ; and he shall be indemnified, by the owner of such land, for any improvements which he shall have made thereon ; the just value of which improvements shall be ascertained by appraisers.

Art. 31.—By will, regulated according to existing laws, or such as may hereafter exist, every new settler, from the day of his establishment, can dispose of his lands, although they shall not be cultivated: and if he shall die intestate, he shall be succeeded in his lands, by the heirs at law of all his property and rights—in either case, the inheritor performing the conditions and obligations of the principal.

Art. 32.—The lands acquired, by virtue of this law, shall, in no case, fall into mortmain ; and those purchasers, who have obtained a title to any, shall not be at liberty to dispose of them, without first having complied with the requisitions of this law.

Art. 33.—A new settler who, in order to establish himself in a foreign country, determines to leave the territory of the State, may do so freely, with all his property; but when once withdrawn, shall no longer hold his lands. And if he shall not before have disposed of them, or if the disposition be not in conformity to Article 19, they shall remain vacated entirely.

Art. 34.—The Government, in agreement with the ordinary ecclesiastics, will be careful to provide an adequate number of Pastors for the new settlements; and in concurrence with the same authority, shall propose to the Legislature for its approbation, the salaries which the said Pastors ought to receive, which are to be paid by the new settlers.

Art. 35.—The new settlers, in regard to the introduction of Slaves, shall be subject to laws which now exist, and which shall hereafter be made on the subject.

Art. 36.—The servants and laborers which, in future, foreign colonists shall introduce, shall not, by force of any contract whatever, remain bound to their service a longer space of time than ten years.

Art. 37.—The commissioner, or commissioners, which shall be appointed in conformity with this law, shall not be suspended in their functions by any other authority than that of the Government. The Judges, within their own jurisdictions respectively, shall inform of any bad management that may be known.

ART. 38.—The Decree of 24th March, 1825, No. 26, is abrogated.

The Governor of the State will understand that this law be complied with:—and he will print, publish, and circulate it.

Given in the city of Leona Vicario, 28th April, 1832.

JOSE JESUS GRANDE,
President.
For MANUEL MUSQIZ, *Secretary.*
CESARIO FIGUERO, *Sec. pro. tem.*

Whereupon, I command that it be printed, published, and circulated; and that it be complied with.

JOSE MARIA DE LETONA.
SANTIGO DEL VALLE, *Secretary.*

Leona Vicario, *May 2d,* 1832.

The land-speculations, aforesaid, have extended to most of the cities and villages of the United States, the British colonies in America, and the settlements of foreigners in all the eastern parts of Mexico. All concerned in them are aware that a change in the government of the country *must* take place, if their claims shall ever be legalized.

The advocates of slavery, in our southern states and elsewhere, want more land on this continent suitable for the culture of sugar and cotton; and if Texas, with the adjoining portions of Tamaulipas, Coahuila, Chihuahua, and Santa Fe, east of the Rio Bravo del Norte, can be wrested from the Mexican government, room will be afforded for the redundant slave population in the United States, even to a remote period of time. The following may be taken as a fair estimate of this extensive region, in square miles, and in English acres. It is calculated from the boundaries of the different departments, as marked in Tanner's Map of Mexico, revised in 1834:—

		Sq. Miles.	Eng. Acres.
Texas, (proper,)		165,000	104,560,000
Tamaulipas east of Rio Bravo,		13,000	8,960,000
Coahuila,	do.	7,000	4,480,000
Chihuahua,	do.	9,000	5,760,000
Santa Fe,	do.	107,000	68,480,000
	Total,	301,000	192,240,000

The breeders of slaves, in those parts of the United States where slave labor has become unprofitable,—and also the traffickers in human flesh, whether American or foreign, desire an extended market, which Texas would afford if revolutionized, and governed as well as inhabited by those who are in favor of re-establishing the system of slavery in that section of country. The northern land-speculators most cheerfully co-operate with the southern slaveholders in the grand scheme of aggression, with the hope of immense gain; and the slave-merchants play into the hands of both, with the same heartless, avaricious feelings and views. The principal seat of operations, for the first, is New York,—though some active and regular agencies are

established at New Orleans and Nashville, and minor agencies in other places. The second exercise their influence individually, without any particular organization: while the third co-operate with all, as opportunities present themselves. They have subsidized presses at command, ready to give extensive circulation to whatever they may wish to publish in furtherance of their views. And orators, legislators, and persons holding official stations under our Federal government, are deeply interested in their operations, and frequently willing instruments to promote their cause.

Such are the motives for action—such the combination of interests—such the organization, sources of influence, and foundation of authority, upon which the present *Texas Insurrection* rests. The resident colonists compose but a small fraction of the party concerned in it. The standard of revolt was raised as soon as it was clearly ascertained that slavery could not be perpetuated, nor the illegal speculations in land continued, under the government of the Mexican Republic. The Mexican authorities were charged with acts of oppression, while the true causes of the revolt—the motives and designs of the insurgents—were studiously concealed from the public view. Influential slaveholders are contributing money, equipping troops, and marching to the scene of conflict. The land speculators are fitting out expeditions from New York and New Orleans, with men, munitions of war, provisions, &c., to promote the object. The Independence of Texas is declared, and the system of slavery, as well as the slave trade, (with the United States,) is fully recognised by the government they have set up. Commissioners are sent from the colonies, and agents are appointed here, to make formal application, enlist the sympathies of our citizens, and solicit aid in every way that it can be furnished. The *hireling presses* are actively engaged in promoting the success of their efforts, by misrepresenting the character of the Mexicans,[*] issuing inflammatory appeals, and urging forward the ignorant, the unsuspecting, the adventurous, and the unprincipled, to a participation in the struggle.

[*] For the purpose of exciting the *sympathy* of the people of the United States, the marauders who are engaged in the Texas insurrection have represented the Mexicans as a blood-thirsty race; while they have themselves, by their *piratical* acts, excited the vengeance of a people with whom their own government is professedly at peace. Some instances of severe retribution have been visited upon them; but most, if not all, of the charges preferred against the Mexicans, as respects their faithlessness and cruelty, are sheer falsehoods. Much has been said about the execution of Fanin and his band of Georgia volunteers. By the *laws* of Mexico (which had been published in this country before they left home) they were considered precisely in the light of pirates. The laws of nations who treated them in the same light, and they were treated accordingly. In a moral view, this was their true character—for their chief object was oppression and the plunder of a people who had never offended them. We have been told that terms of capitulation were granted them, by which their lives were to be spared. This the Mexican Generals have promptly and positively denied; and we have more reason to credit their assertions, than those engaged in piratical enterprises.

4

In the course of my observations, I have several times asserted, that it was the intention of the insurrectionists to establish and perpetuate the system of slavery, by " *Constitutional*" provision. In proof of this, I now quote several paragraphs from the Constitution which they lately adopted. This extract is taken from that part under the head of " General Provisions," and embraces all that relates to slavery. We remember the proclamation of D. G. Burnet, the President of their assumed government, issued a few months since, setting forth that their Constitution *prohibited the "slave trade,"* &c.* That " proclamation " was circulated for the special purpose of deceiving the opponents of slavery in the United States and inducing them to join in their marauding crusade. It will now be seen, that the measure was a device of the most hypocritical complexion. This extract will also be found to contain much that is fully confirmatory of what I have before stated, upon other topics connected with the general subject before us.

SEC. 6. All free white persons who shall emigrate to this Republic, and who shall, after a residence of six months, make oath before some competent authority that he intends to reside permanently in the same, and shall swear to support this Constitution, and that he will bear true allegiance to the Republic of Texas, shall be entitled to all the privileges of citizenship.

SEC. 7. So soon as convenience will permit, there shall be a penal code formed on principles of reformation, and not of vindictive justice; ard the civil and criminal laws shall be revised, digested, and arranged under different heads; and all laws relating to land titles shall be translated, revised, and promulgated.

SEC. 8. All persons who shall leave the country for the purpose of evading a participation in the present struggle, *or shall refuse to participate in it,* or shall give aid or assistance to the present enemy, *shall forfeit all rights to citizenship, and such lands as they may hold, in the Republic.*

SEC. 9. All persons of color, who were slaves for life, previous to their emigration to Texas, and who *are now held in bondage,* shall remain in the like state of servitude, provided the said slave shall be the bona fide property of the person so holding said slave as aforesaid. *Congress shall pass no laws to prohibit emigrants from the United States of America from bringing their slaves into the Republic with them,* and holding them by the same tenure by which such slaves were held in the United States; *nor shall Congress have the power to emancipate slaves; nor shall any slaveholder be allowed to emancipate his or her slave or slaves, without the consent of Congress,* unless he or she shall send his or her slave or slaves without the limits of the Republic. No *free* person of African descent, either in

whole or in part, shall *be permitted to reside permanently in the Republic,* without the consent of Congress; and the importation or admission of Africans or negroes into this Republic, excepting from the United States of America, is forever prohibited, and declared to be piracy.

SEC. 10. All persons, (*Africans, the descendants of Africans, and Indians excepted,*) who were residing in Texas on the day of the Declaration of Independence, [A great portion of the *native Mexican citizens* are, of course, *excluded!*] shall be considered citizens of the Republic, and entitled to all the privileges of such. All citizens now living in Texas who have not received their portion of land, in like manner as colonists, shall be entitled to their land in the following proportion and manner: Every head of a family shall be entitled to one league and "labor" of land, and every single man of the age of seventeen and upwards, shall be entitled to the third part of one league of land. All citizens who may have, previously to the adoption of this Constitution, received their league of land as heads of families, and their quarter of a league of land as single persons, shall receive such additional quantity as will make the quantity of land received by them equal to one league and "labor," and one-third of a league, unless by bargain, sale, or exchange, they have transferred, or may henceforth transfer their right to said land, or a portion thereof, to some other citizen of the Republic; and in such case the person to whom such right shall have been transferred, shall be entitled to the same, as fully and amply as the person making the transfer might or could have been. No alien shall hold land in Texas, except by titles emanating directly from the Government of this Republic. But if any citizen of this Republic should die intestate or otherwise, his children or heirs shall inherit his estate, and aliens shall have a reasonable time to take possession of and dispose of the same, in a manner hereinafter to be pointed out by law. Orphan children whose parents were entitled to land under the colonization law of Mexico, and who now reside in the Republic, shall be entitled to all the rights of which their parents were possessed at the time of their death. The citizens of the Republic shall not be compelled to reside on the land, but shall have their lines plainly marked.

All orders of survey legally obtained by any citizen of the Republic, from any legally authorized commissioner, prior to the act of the late consultation closing the land offices, shall be valid. In all cases the actual settler and occupant of the soil shall be entitled, in locating his land, to include his improvement, in preference to all other claims not acquired previous to his settlement, according to the law of the land and this Constitution: *Provided,* That nothing herein contained shall prejudice the rights of any citizen from whom a settler may hold land by rent or lease.

And whereas the protection of the public domain from unjust and fraudulent claims, and quieting the people in the enjoyment of their lands is one of the great duties of this great Convention: and whereas the Legislature of the State of Coahuila & Texas having passed an act in the year eighteen hundred and thirty-four, in behalf of General John T. Mason, of New York, and another on the fourteenth day of March, eighteen hundred and thirty-five, *under which the enormous amount of eleven hundred leagues of land has been claimed by sundry individuals, some of whom reside in foreign countries, and are not citizens of the Republic, which said acts are contrary to articles fourth, twelfth, and fifteenth of the laws of eighteen hundred and*

---

* When the Convention (so called) was assembled at San Felipe to draft a State Constitution, David G. Burnet introduced the resolution condemning the Cuba slave trader, to which I have before adverted. Then, as now, he wished to *save appearances;* and he succeeded in obtaining a majority to sustain his resolution. But I learned from one of the members of that body, that it was violently opposed by some of them, and passed with difficulty. During the discussion, a motion was offered to *throw it under the table.* This was strenuously advocated—while one, in the fervor of his "republican" patriotism, loudly exclaimed: " *Throw it into H——*" !!

twenty-four, of the General Congress of Mexico, and one of the said acts for that cause has, by the said General Congress of Mexico, been declared null and void: it is hereby declared that the said act of eighteen hundred and thirty-four, in favour of John T. Mason, and of the fourteenth of March, eighteen hundred and thirty-five, of the said Legislature of Coahuila & Texas, and each and every grant founded thereon, is, and was from the beginning, null and void; and all surveys made under pretence of authority derived from said acts are hereby declared to be null and void; and all eleven-league claims, located within twenty leagues of the boundary line between Texas and the United States of America, which have been located contrary to the laws of Mexico, are hereby declared to be null and void: and whereas many surveys and titles to land have been made while most of the people of Texas were absent from home, serving in the campaign against Bejar, it is hereby declared that all the surveys and locations of land made since the act of the late consultation closing the land offices, and all titles to land made since that time, are and shall be null and void.

The adoption of a Constitution with such provisions as are here quoted, may be termed the crowning act—the finishing stroke of this monstrous scheme of oppression, so far as the expressed will of those concerned in it can be manifested by conventional regulation. When we look back to the commencement of their operations, and trace their movements step by step, bearing in mind their open declarations upon various occasions, what man of reason and common sense can, for one moment, doubt that the re-establishment of Slavery has been their principal object, their settled determination, from the beginning? I think it will be admitted, by every person of penetration, reflection, and unbiassed judgment, that the evidence I have produced is conclusive on this point. I might state many more facts and circumstances, which have come to my knowledge during a long and intimate acquaintance with their proceedings, all tending to the same conclusion. My intercourse with many of the actors in the great drama, has given me numerous opportunities to understand their motives and their designs. It is indeed impossible that I should be mistaken in the one or the other. And as unfolding events coincide fully with my assertions, and with the proofs already adduced to sustain them, it might be considered unnecessary to dwell longer upon this particular topic. Yet, in order that the reader may lack no important information, that will show the decided stand which the Mexican government has taken against the toleration of slavery, I will quote a few more official documents (to some of which I have heretofore alluded) in verification of what I have asserted, and already perhaps sufficiently proved.

The following decrees and ordinances are translated from an official compilation, published by authority of the Mexican Government, embracing all the public acts of said government from the period of its organization to the year 1830.—

DECREE OF JULY 13, 1824.

Prohibition of the Commerce and Traffic in Slaves.

The Sovereign General Constituent Congress of the United Mexican States has held it right to decree the following:

1. The Commerce and Traffic in Slaves, proceeding from whatever power, and under whatever flag, is forever prohibited, within the territories of the United Mexican States.

2. The Slaves, who may be introduced contrary to the tenor of the preceding article, shall remain free in consequence of treading the Mexican soil.

3. Every vessel, whether National or Foreign, in which Slaves may be transported and introduced into the Mexican territories, shall be confiscated with the rest of its cargo—and the Owner, Purchaser, Captain, Master, and Pilot, shall suffer the punishment of ten years confinement.

4. This law will take effect from the date of its publication; however, as to the punishments prescribed in the preceding article, they shall not take effect till six months after, towards the Planters who, in virtue of the law of the 14th October last, relating to the Colonization of the Isthmus of Guazacoalco, and may disembark Slaves for the purpose of introducing them into the Mexican territory.

(See the 21st article of the Decree of October 11, 1823.)

DECREE

Of the 18th of December, 1824, upon Colonization.

The Sovereign General Constituent Congress of the United States of Mexico, have resolved and do fully decree:

1. The Mexican nation offers to Foreigners who come to establish themselves in their territory, security in their persons and in their property, provided they subject themselves to the laws of the country.

2. This law applies to those territories of the nation which, not being individual property nor belonging to any Corporation or Town, may be colonized.

3. For this purpose the Congresses of the States will form, with the greatest brevity, the laws or regulations of colonization, of their respective demarcation, conforming themselves in all cases to the regulations established by this law.

4. It is not permitted to colonize the territories within twenty leagues of the boundaries of any foreign nation, nor within ten leagues bordering on the sea coast, without the previous approbation of the supreme general executive power.

5. If, for the defence or security of the nation, the Government of the Federation should find it convenient to make use of some portion of these lands, to construct magazines, arsenals, or other public buildings, the same may be verified with the approbation of the general Congress, or during its recess with that of the Council of Government.

6. It is not permitted before four years from the publication of this Law, to impose any duty upon the importations, for their own use, by foreigners, who may establish themselves for the first time in the country.

7. Before the year 1840 the general Congress cannot prohibit the entrance of foreigners, to colonize, unless imperious circumstances oblige them to do so with respect to individuals of any nation.

8. The Government without prejudice to the

object of this law, shall take, in regard to the foreign-ers who come to colonize, the precautions which they may judge suitable for the security of the Federation.

9. A preference must be attended to in the distribution of lands to the Mexican citizens; and no distinction must be made betwixt them except what particular merit and services done to the country, may give them a right to. Circumstances being equal, a preference will be given to those who have lands in the neighborhood of the territory to be distributed.

10. The Military who, with reference to the offer of the 27th March 1821, may hold a right to lands, shall be attended to in the States, on shewing the certificates which the superior executive power may have given them for this purpose.

11. If by the decrees of capitulation according to the probabilities of life the supreme executive power should find it convenient to alienate certain portions of land in favor of certain Officers of the Federation whether military or civil, the same may be ratified in the registers of the territory.

12. It is not permitted that there should be held in property, by one individual, more than one square league of five thousand rods of meadow land, four of secular land, six of pasture.

13. The new settlers are not permitted to leave their property in entail.

14. This Law guarantees the contracts which "Empresarios" may have made with the families whom they bring on at their own expense; it being always understood that these contracts are not contrary to the laws.

15. No one who, by virtue of this law may acquire landed property, can preserve it if settled permanently out of the territories of the republic.

16. The government, in conformity with the principles established in this Law, shall proceed to the colonization of the territories of the Republic.

(See the order of the 11th April, 1823, and the Decree of the 14th October, 1823.)

[Translated from Vol. 2., page 94. Mexican Laws.]

NOTE. In an order of the 11th of April, [1823] notice is given to government that if it find no inconvenience, it may yield to the solicitation of Stephen F. Austin, in confirming to him the Grant for settling Three Hundred families in Texas, and it can moreover, decide upon other applications of a similar nature, and cause to be suspended till further determination, the law of Colonization enacted by the *Junta Instituyente.*

[Translated from Vol. 2 , page 199, Mexican Laws.]

Extract from the Law of 14th October, 1823.

ART. 21. Foreigners who bring slaves with them, shall obey the laws established upon the matter, or which shall hereafter be established.

(See the Decree of 13th July, 1824.)

[Translated from Vol. 5., page 149., Mexican Laws.]

DECREE OF PRESIDENT GUERRERO.

Abolition of Slavery.

The President of the United Mexican States, to the inhabitants of the Republic:—

Be it known: That in the year 1829, being desirous of signalizing the anniversary of our Independence by an act of national Justice and Beneficence, which may contribute to the strength and support of such inestimable welfare, as to secure more and more the public tranquillity, and reinstate an unfortunate portion of our inhabitants in the sacred rights granted them by nature, and may be protected by the nation under wise and just laws, according to the provision in Article 30, of the Constitutive Act ; availing myself of the extraordinary faculties granted me, I have thought proper to Decree :

1. That Slavery be exterminated in the Republic.

2. Consequently those are free, who, up to this day, have been looked upon as slaves.

3. Whenever the circumstances of the Public Treasury will allow it, the owners of slaves shall be indemnified, in the manner which the Laws shall provide.

JOSE MARIA DE BOCANEGRA. *Mexico,* 15*th Sept.,* 1829, A. D.

[Translation of part of the law of April 6th, 1830, prohibiting the migration of citizens of the United States to Texas.]

ARTICLE 9.—On the northern frontier the entrance of foreigners shall be prohibited, under all pretexts whatever, unless they be furnished with passports, signed by the agents of the Republic, at the places whence they proceed.

ART. 10.—There shall be no variation with regard to the colonies already established, nor with regard to the slaves that may be in them ; but the General Government, or the particular State Government, *shall take care, under the strictest responsibility, that the colonization laws be obeyed, and that no more slaves be introduced.*

ART. 11.—In use of the power reserved by the General Congress in the 7th Article of the law of August 18th, 1824, it is prohibited to neighboring nations to settle in those States and Territories of the federation which border on their nations. Consequently, contracts which have not been executed, and are opposed to that law, shall be superseded.

I have said that the present contest in Texas has assumed a character which must seriously affect both the interests and the honor of this nation; and that the policy and measures of the government are deeply involved in it. I do not say that the government has *officially* committed itself upon the question.—This has been most studiously avoided, while it has been completely under the influence of the "*Combination*" engaged in the outrageous "crusade," and has given *efficient aid* by a tacit acquiescence therein, as far as it could possibly be done consistently with the preservation of even the shadow of "neutrality."

When a Mexican national vessel was taken into New Orleans, by the piratical expedition from that place, a mere *mock-trial* was instituted against those violators of our treaty with Mexico and the law of nations. Armed bands have been *permitted* to proceed from different parts of the United States *openly* and *avowedly*, to join in the contest, without the least degree of molestation; and even when complaints have been officially made by accredited Mexican agents, nothing has been done to arrest them except the *formal* transmission of orders to the District Attorneys, to which they paid not the slightest attention.

In addition to this positive neglect or refusal

to enforce the neutral obligations of the nation, a claim has been set up—(a claim the most preposterous that can be imagined—) to a large extent of Mexican territory, with the view of placing an armed force in the vicinity of the combatants, to over-awe the Mexican troops and afford opportunities to aid the insurgents.*

A false construction also has been given to a clause in the treaty between the two governments, in relation to the restriction of the Indian tribes within their respective limits, by virtue of which a large force has been ordered to the frontiers under the *pretence* of enforcing the provisions of said treaty. It is well understood that these troops, collected from among the advocates of slavery in the south-western States, will not remain inactive, "neutral" spectators, when the crisis arrives in which their participation in the contest may be desirable to the instigators of the war. I do not stand alone in the view which is here taken of the subject. By a reference to the speech of John Quincy Adams, from which I shall hereafter make some extracts, it will be seen that similar ideas are expressed by him; and it may be added, that many of the most intelligent men among us are fully convinced of their general correctness.

The following is the Article in the Treaty, under the authority of which our Government has instructed General Gaines to cross the boundary line. Who can perceive the warrant that it is supposed to give either party, to go beyond the limits of its own territory with an armed force?—And further,—what authority does it give either, to prevent the Indians from joining the one or the other, *as friendly allies?*

"ART. 33. It is likewise agreed that the two contracting parties shall, by all the means in their power, maintain peace and harmony among the several Indian nations who inhabit the lands adjacent to the lines and rivers which form the boundaries of the two countries; and the better to attain this object, both parties bind themselves expressly to restrain, by force, all hostilities and incursions on the part of the Indian nations being within their respective boundaries: so that the United States of America will not suffer their Indians to attack the citizens of the United Mexican States, nor the Indians inhabiting their territory; nor will the United Mexican States permit the Indians residing within their territories to commit hostilities against the citizens of the United States of America, nor against the Indians residing within the limits of the United States in any manner whatever.

And in the event of any person or persons captured by the Indians who inhabit the territory of either of the contracting parties, being or having been carried into the territories of the other, both Governments engage and bind themselves in the most solemn manner to return them to their country, as soon as they know of their being within their respective territories, or to deliver them up to the agent or representative of the Government that claims them; giving

to each other, reciprocally, timely notice, and the claimant paying the expenses incurred in the transmission and maintenance of such person or persons, who, in the meantime, shall be treated with the utmost hospitality by the local authorities of the place where they may be.—Nor shall it be lawful, under any pretext whatever, for the citizens of either of the contracting parties to purchase or hold captive prisoners made by the Indians inhabiting the territories of the other."

Under the erroneous construction of the treaty, aforesaid, General Gaines was authorized to cross the boundary line with his army; to *march seventy miles* into the Mexican territory; and to occupy the military post of Nacogdoches, *in case he should judge it expedient in order to guard against Indian depredations!* —And further, he was likewise authorized to call upon the Governors of several of the *south-western States* for an additional number of troops, *should he consider it* necessary.

In order to furnish an excuse for the exercise of the authority thus delegated to him, many false rumours of Indian depredations and hostile movements were reported to the Commander of the United States forces, and he did not neglect the occasion for pushing to the *very extent* of his *conditional* instructions.—(His proceedings in this case are of so recent date, that they must be familiar to every intelligent reader, and need not be here specified.)—He even went so far that the Executive became alarmed, *lest the "neutrality" of our Government should be violated!!*—and his requisitions upon the governors of Tennessee and Kentucky were countermanded. Yet he is still permitted to keep an imposing force stationed in the Mexican territory; and it is understood that he is in regular correspondence with the chiefs of the insurgent armies; also that his men are "deserting" and joining them in great numbers.*

The insurrectionists are thus indirectly encouraged, and *assisted*, by our Government.—And the hope is entertained, by those concerned, that the efforts of the Mexicans may be thus paralyzed, and the possession of the territory retained by the revolutionists, until the next meeting of the Congress of the United States, when the independence of the *Texian Republic* may be formally acknowledged, and soon thereafter admitted, as an "Independent State," into this confederacy. This the "Combination" is fully determined upon. It is the

---

* One of the deep laid plans of the *combination* was, to send their "volunteers" to the frontier, through the agency and *at the expense* of the government.

---

* In stating these facts, it may be well to accompany them with the *proof*—and here it is.—How well the plan is devised!—How completely the system works!—What undeniable evidence, too, of a *strict* "neutrality" on our part!!!

From the Pensacola Gazette.

About the middle of last month, General Gaines sent an officer of the United States army into Texas to reclaim some deserters. He found them already enlisted in the Texian service to the number of *two hundred*. They still wore the uniform of our army, but refused, of course, to return. The commander of the Texian forces, was applied to, to enforce their return; but his only reply was, that the soldiers might go, but he had no authority to send them back. This is a new view of our Texian relations.

ultimatum of their grand design. I repeat that its *members have a majority in the councils of the nation;* and as the sentiments of the Executive Head coincides with theirs, *the government is completely under their controlling influence;* and their object will certainly be accomplished, UNLESS THE PEOPLE OF OUR FREE STATES AROUSE FROM THEIR APATHY, and by an open, decided, general expression of their sentiments, induce their Senators and Representatives in Congress to oppose the measure.

It is indeed astonishing, that many intelligent persons in this country have so long suffered themselves to be blinded and deceived, in relation to this subject. I am aware that the parties to the unholy compact have uniformly veiled their designs with specious pretexts and systematic misrepresentations. But within the last few months, particularly, they have nearly thrown off the mask. Their cloak is a mere veil of gauze; and we have nothing to do but open our eyes, to perceive the hideous reality of the corruption beneath it.

Although it has been generally asserted, and many have been induced to believe, that the only object of the insurrectionists is the establishment of an *independent* government, separate from that of any other,—yet the principal original advocates of the scheme— the *slaveholders, slave-breeders,* and *politicians* of the United States—never entertained the idea for a moment. The land speculators and *foreign* slave-traders would have no objection to it; (neither would the colonists object to it;) but they could not expect to effect the alienation of the territory from the Mexican Government without the aid, either directly or indirectly, of the Government of the United States. This aid could not be obtained, without the prospect of the future attachment of the territory to this Confederation, *to increase the power and preponderating influence of the slaveholding States in the National Congress.* The plan of establishing an "Independent Republic" in Texas was, therefore, publicly proclaimed, first, with the view of effectually separating the territory from Mexico, and firmly re-establishing slavery; and, secondly, to bring it into this Union without subjecting our Government to the charge of official interference in the accomplishment of those objects. *No other plan would have succeeded;* while this has deceived the opponents of slavery, lulled them into a fatal security, and thrown them entirely off their guard, as it respects their own interests and safety. So far as the "combination" has succeeded in establishing its authority, the territory is wrested from Mexico; the system of slavery, and the slave-trade with this country, are fully recognized; and all the necessary preliminaries are arranged for the formal sanction of independence and admission into the ranks of the sovereign slaveholding States composing this Republic, at an early day. This, too, has all been done with the

connivance and aid of our Government, *without formally violating its " neutrality!"*

If there are any who yet doubt the intentions of the insurgents, respecting the attachment of the territory in question to that of the United States, they are particularly requested to read what follows,—and a moment's reflection will probably then satisfy them of the truth of the averment. It will be perceived that even Stephen F. Austin himself *now* sanctions it openly.

By the recent arrival of a vessel from one of the ports in Texas, a paper bearing date the 9th of August has been received from that country, in which an election for officers of their Government is announced to be held in a short time. Stephen F. Austin is one of the candidates for the Presidency; and in a letter published in the paper aforesaid, he expresses himself thus:—

                    Columbia, August 4th, 1836.

DEAR SIR:—I have been nominated by many persons whose opinions I am bound to respect, as a candidate for the office of President of Texas, at the September elections.

Influenced by the great governing principle which has regulated my actions since I came to Texas, fifteen years ago, which is, to serve this country in any capacity in which the people might think proper to employ me, I shall not decline the highly responsible and difficult one now proposed, should the majority of my fellow citizens elect me.

I perceive by the proclamation of the President, ordering the election, that the people are requested to say whether they are in favor, or not, of annexing Texas to the United States. On this point, I shall consider myself bound, if elected, to obey the will of the people. As a citizen, however, I am free to say, *that I am in favor of annexation, and will do all in my power to effect it with the least possible delay.*

          Respectfully,
               Your fellow Citizen,
                         S. F. AUSTIN.

The same paper contains the following enunciation from William H. Jack, who recently officiated as their Secretary of State, but is now proposed as a candidate for the Legislature. He writes in answer to sundry interrogatories from those who put him in nomination;—and after replying to three other questions, unconnected with the subject before us, he concludes as follows:—

Fourth. I am decidedly and anxiously in favor of annexing Texas to the United States. I consider it the "*rock of our salvation,*" and a consummation of happiness "most devoutly to be wished for." Should I be chosen a representative to Congress, I shall leave no effort untried to produce this desired object, feeling confident, that all the blessings of peace and tranquillity will thereby be secured, to ourselves and our posterity.

Fifth. When I first read the Constitution, as adopted by the Convention, I was of opinion that some errors had crept into it, and hence was in favor of submitting to the people, whether they would adopt it absolutely, or clothe Congress with powers to amend it.

Subsequent reflection, and the importance of organizing a constitutional government immediately, have satisfied me that it ought to be adopted, as it now stands; believing that in the present unsettled state of the country, less injury will result from its adoption than by making amendments at this time.

Thus, gentlemen, I have answered every question proposed, and if my views are conformable to those of the people of this jurisdiction, and they should think proper to elect me, I shall serve them fearlessly and faithfully.

I am, very respectfully,
Your obedient servant,
WILLIAM H. JACK.

Columbia, 5th August, 1836.

Hear, also, the language of General Houston. The following is from a late number of the Washington Globe.

"GENERAL HOUSTON.—The opinion of General Houston is, that Texas, when it shall have asserted its independence, will seek admission into the Union. He is, himself, decidedly in favor of that course, considering it *essential to the interests of the new country, and of much importance to the Union.*"

Notwithstanding that Stephen F. Austin (and I may add many other *actual settlers* in Texas) would have preferred a separate *independent* Government, we now see that they have no expectation of establishing one. On the contrary, they unequivocally declare the intention of annexing the country to the United States, as soon as it can possibly be done. They could not exercise their will in the matter. *The great majority of the fomentors of the rebellion, and the immediate participators in it,* ARE CITIZENS OF THIS COUNTRY. Such of the colonists as were opposed to it, however, have been *compelled* to acquiesce, and the agents of the "Combination" have successfully dictated its prescribed measures, and pursued the course originally contemplated by it.

I will add a few more facts, collected from various sources, to those already enumerated, tending to prove the determination of southern slaveholders to acquire the Texas country, *for the purpose* of re-establishing Slavery, and annexing the territory to the United States, as aforesaid.

A gentleman of intelligence and veracity residing in Ohio, formerly a member of the Legislature of that State, recently visited the south-western country, and gives the result of his observations upon this particular subject, in a letter to the editor of the *National Enquirer,* as follows:—

"I have read the pamphlet entitled 'The Origin and true Causes of the Texas Insurrection.'* I was abundantly satisfied on this point before I saw it. No secret is made of it on the Ohio and Mississippi—it is openly avowed, and warmly defended. The colder slave countries feel themselves very deeply interested, and now think of *breeding slaves* in earnest. Men and money will be liberally furnished. Numerous Kentuckians—young men, ambitious of fame, and seeking fortunes—will even go from Illinois, where they had previously emigrated."

Another very respectable gentleman, who

* A pamphlet containing a series of essays over the signature of "Columbus," by the author of this. The essays, alluded to, were first published in the Philadelphia *National Gazette,* in the winter of 1835.

lately travelled with the Hon. Mr. Peyton, of Tennessee, informs us that this distinguished *member of Congress* unhesitatingly expressed his determination to use his influence in procuring the annexation of Texas to the United States, in order that a number more slave states may be created and admitted into the Union, to preserve the preponderance of slaveholding influence and power in the government.

The following items, extracted from *late* newspapers, may very properly be noticed and borne in mind. The "United States Telegraph," published at Washington City, says:—

"It is stated, on unquestionable authority, that a letter was found among the papers of the late Huchins G. Burton, Ex-Governor of North Carolina, from a person high in authority, stating that Texas would certainly be annexed to the United States,—at the same time offering to make him (Burton) Governor of said Territory. If the statement be true, and we do not doubt it, what a state of things does it disclose!!"

The Telegraph proceeds to argue, that the object of the "person high in authority," was to obtain the *political influence* of Governor Burton, in the coming election contest. We have not a shadow of doubt respecting the truth of the statement. We have heard it frequently, and can trace it to unquestionably authentic sources. Some noise has also been made about it, recently, in the newspapers. But the subject is not more connected with politics, than with the long meditated, now operative, attempt to provide for the *extension of slavery* to that part of the continent.

The "Mobile Advertiser," of a recent date, holds forth this emphatic language:—

"The South wish to have Texas admitted into the Union for two reasons: First, to equalize the South with the North; and secondly, as a convenient and safe place, calculated from its peculiarly good soil and salubrious climate, for a slave population. Interest and political safety both, alike prompt the action and enforce the argument. The South contends that preservation and justice to themselves call for that aid to be tendered to them which would be given by the acquisition of Texas. They are not safe as they are. They are not balanced with the free states. Their exposure to insurrection is fourfold, with not one-fourth the means to redress their grievances. They contend that they have an internal foe within, and an awful foe in all those who demand the emancipation of their slaves, and who call upon them to give up their property now and for ever. The question is therefore put by the South to Congress and the country, 'Shall we have justice done us by the admission of Texas into the Union, whenever that admission may be asked by the Texians themselves?' The question is a fair one, and must soon be met by Congress and the nation. The North almost to a man will answer NO. The West will be divided, and the discussion of the question will find two strong and powerful parties; the one in favor of Texas, a slaveholding province, and the other against it."

To the foregoing we subjoin a *toast,* lately

given at a public meeting of eminent politicians, at Columbia, South Carolina:—

"TEXAS—If united to our government as a state,
it will prove an invaluable acquisition to the southern
states, and their domestic institutions."

Notices, of the following purport, are very
frequently to be seen in the southern and
south-western papers. This is copied from a
North Carolina Journal.

"WHO WILL GO TO TEXAS?

Major J. H. Harry, of Lincolnton, has been au-
thorised by me, with the consent of Major General
Hunt, an agent in the western counties of North
Carolina, to receive and enrol Volunteer emigrants
to Texas, and will conduct such as may wish to emigrate to that Republic, about the first of October
next, at the expense of the Republic of Texas.

J. P. HENDERSON,
Brig. Gen'l. of Texian Army.
August, 1836."

The paragraph below, gives us a view of
operations upon a pretty large scale; and
while we peruse it, we must recollect, that no
measures have been taken by our government, to
prevent this bold and glaring violation of our
own laws and the integrity of the Mexican
Republic!

THREE HUNDRED MEN FOR TEXAS.—General
Dunlap, of Tennessee, is about to proceed to Texas
with the above number of men. The whole corps
are now at Memphis. They will not, it is said, pass
this way. Every man is completely armed, the
corps having been originally raised for the Florida
war. This force, we have no doubt, will be able to
carry every thing before it.—*Vicksburg Register*.

It is gratifying to learn, that the motives of
those engaged in this outrageous Crusade are
beginning to be understood and justly appreciated, by some of the most intelligent citizens
of the United States.

A gentleman of great philanthropy, intelligence, and public spirit, in the State of New
York, thus expresses himself in a letter of
recent date:—

"The Texians could have effected nothing, but
for the assistance furnished by the southern states,
who have as fully waged the war they excited, as
though it had been formally declared by them. The
number of respectable men in Texas is too small to
redeem the country and their cause from the fathom-
less abyss of misery, degradation and infamy, into
which the projected establishment and perpetuation
of slavery must inevitably plunge them as well as the
United States. Meanwhile, all the slave-mongers,
slave-politicians, and *slave-presses*, on this side the
Sabine and Red rivers, are using the utmost exertions to force the recognition of Texian Independence,
and its incorporation with the United States as speedily as possible. This monstrous outrage, unsurpassed
in the blackest page of history, is fast tending to its
consummation."

An able writer in the same State, who ranks
among the most eminent legal professional
characters, emphatically remarks as follows,
in a communication to the editor of the *National Enquirer*.—Speaking of the "Texas
Conspiracy," he says:—

"I cannot now bring to my recollection, in the

history of the world, so foul and abominable a conspiracy against the laws of nations, of civil society,
and the rights of man, as this nefarious combination
of land-speculators, land-pirates, and man-stealers,
under the name of *Texian Patriots*, presents:—and
this too in the nineteenth century, and in the midst
of a people who boast of being highly intelligent, and
claim to be the friends of law, order, liberty, and the
RIGHTS OF MAN!!!—From my inmost soul I
sicken at the thought."

The editor of the New York *Sun* quotes an
extract from the letter of General Houston to
General Dunlap, of Nashville, in which he
says:—"For a portion of this force we must
look to the United States. It cannot reach us
too soon. There is but one feeling in Texas,
in my opinion, and that is to establish the independence of Texas, and to be attached to the
United States"—and then remarks:

"Here, then, is an open avowal by the commander
in chief of the Texian army, that American troops
will be required to seize and sever this province of
the Mexican republic, for the purpose of uniting it
to ours; and this avowal is made by a distinguished
American citizen, in the very face of that glorious
constitution of his country, which wisely gives no
power to its citizens for acquiring foreign territory
by conquest, their own territory being more than
amply sufficient to gratify any safe ambition; and in
the face, too, of the following solemn and sacred contract of his country with the sister republic which he
would dismember:—

'There shall be a firm inviolable, and universal
peace, and a true and sincere friendship between the
United States of America, and the United Mexican
States, in all the extent of their possessions and territories, between their people and citizens respectively,
without distinction of persons or places.'

In the earlier days of our republic, when a high-
minded and honorable fidelity to its constitution was
an object proudly paramount to every mercenary
consideration that might contravene it, an avowed
design of this kind against the possessions of a nation
with whom the United States were at peace, would
have subjected its author, if a citizen, to the charge
of high treason, and to its consequences.—When
Aaron Burr and his associates were supposed to
meditate the conquest of Mexico, and attempted to
raise troops in the southern states to achieve it, they
were arrested for treason, and Burr, their chief, was
tried for his life. But now, behold! the conquest
of a part of the same country is an object openly
proclaimed, not in the letters of General Houston
alone, but by many of our wealthiest citizens at public banquets, and by the hireling presses in the chief
cities of our Union. The annexation of a foreign
territory to our own by foreign conquest, being thus
unblushingly avowed, and our citizens who are integral portions of our national sovereignty being openly
invited and incited to join the crusade with weapons
of war, it becomes an interesting moral inquiry—
what is there in the public mind to excuse or even to
palliate so flagrant a prostitution of national faith and
honor in these days, any more than in the days that
are past? The answer is ready at hand, and is
irrefutable. An extensive and well organized gang
of swindlers in Texas lands, have raised the cry, and
the standard of 'Liberty!' and to the thrilling charm
of this glorious word, which stirs the blood of a free
people, as the blast of the bugle arouses every nerve
of the war-horse, have the generous feelings of our
citizens responded in ardent delusion. But, as the

Commercial Advertiser truly declares, 'Never was the Goddess of American Liberty invoked more unrighteously ;' and we cannot but believe that the natural sagacity, good sense, and proud regard for their national honor, for which our citizens are distinguished in the eyes of all nations, will speedily rescue them from the otherwise degrading error in which that vile crew of mercenary, hypocritical swindlers would involve them. The artful deceivers, however, have not relied upon the generosity and noble sympathy only of our fellow-citizens, for they insidiously presented a bribe to excite their cupidity also. They have not only falsely represented the Texian cause as one of pure, disinterested liberty and justice, as opposed to perfidious tyranny and cruel oppression, but they have themselves assumed something more than the liberty which they basely and hypocritically advocate, by impudently promising a fertile paradisaical piece of Texian land, *a mile square*, to every American citizen and foreign emigrant, who will sally forth to capture it from the Mexican republic ! Induced by one or both of these objects, many hundreds of our enterprising citizens left their own ample and unobjectionable country, to unite with Irish, English, and other foreign adventurers in a war, from the fullest success of which, only some six or eight Land Companies, who have fraudulently and audaciously monopolized the Texian territory, would gain an important benefit. And to this shrine of Mammon, concealed by the crowding banners of ostensible liberty, have many hundreds of our gallant youth been treacherously sacrificed—sacrificed by a mercenary treachery, compared to which that exercised by Santa Anna, in defence of the Republic of which he was President, was innocence and patriotism.

Had we in the Texians, a brave and injured people, struggling in the land of their birth, or even o. their adopted, for those abstract and social rights o. mankind which were the objects of *our* revolution, and which *we* obtained and enjoy, theirs would be a cause with which angels might sympathize, and which the bolts of heaven might well be launched to aid. But is it such a cause ?—Deceived by misrepresentations, we were ourselves led so to consider it, in its earlier efforts; but a fair examination of facts has undeceived us, and we look in vain either for such a cause or such a people in the Texians. What are the facts?

We pledge ourselves to answer the question with a perspicuity which shall defy all future obscuration, and with a rigid adherence to truth which shall defy the most desperate efforts to refute We have, at present, only room to state, in brief, that the Texian revolution was concerted by the planters and slave speculators in the southern states ever since the first permission given by the Spanish authorities to Moses Austin of Missouri, in the year 1820, to introduce 300 families, professing the Catholic religion, as colonists of a grant of land which he obtained on this express condition. From that time to the present moment the aggressions have been on the part of the colonists, under the sanction of the southern speculators; and not until their purpose of getting a physical force into the province which shou ld detach it from Mexico, and make it a slaveholding state, became flagrant and undisguised, had the settlers ever received aught but protection, encouragement, toleration and kindness, from the Mexican government. They paid no taxes, had their own laws and tribunals, were allowed to profess and exercise all the religions they chose, though contrary to the Mexican constitution, enjoyed all the fruits of a beautiful and bounteous soil without return or tribute to the government to which it belonged, and were, without

exception, the freest civilized people upon the face of the earth. But the object of the colonizing land agents of the South was to make this prolific province their own and the field of a new and lucrative negro slavery. To this they still tenaciously adhere; and if they can induce a strong force of our American youth to shed their blood for the unjust and avaricious cause of slavery, under the name of Texian liberty and independence, they will undoubtedly secure their object. We doubt not the ability of our gallant countrymen to exterminate any number of Mexicans that can be brought against them; but in fighting for the union of Texas with the United States, which is the avowed meaning of "Texian Independence," they will be fighting for that which, at no distant period, will inevitably DI SOLVE THE UNION. The slave states having this eligible addition to their land of bondage, with its harbors, bays, and well-bounded geographical position, will ere long cut asunder the federal tie which they have long held with ungracious and unfraternal fingers, and confederate a new and distinct slaveholding republic, in opposition to the whole free republic of the North. Thus early will be fulfilled the prediction of the old politicians of Europe, that our Union could not remain one century entire—and then also will the maxim be exemplified in our history, as it is in the history of the slaveholding repub'ics of old, that liberty and slavery cannot long inhabit the same soil."

Many more extracts might be taken from the newspapers, &c , advancing similar opinions and arguments. There can be no mistake in these indications of an awakening spirit among the virtuous and intelligent of our counmen ; and it is to be hoped that the NORTHERN PRESS, at least, will soon be roused to action. The great question is: will it be so general as to arrest the grand marplots in their unholy career, before the seal shall have been set to their abominable project? Let the PUBLIC VOICE BE RAISED IN TONES OF THUNDER, from the shores of the Atlantic to our inland seas, and from the mountain forests of Maine to the swamps of Louisiana.—Let the nation be *thoroughly* awakened, and all may yet be well.—Otherwise, the Demon of Oppression will triumph, and our children must wear his chains—or blood will flow in torrents, and the land will be drenched with their crimson gore!

I have now traced the subject of the *Texian Revolt* through the whole concatenation of its primary causes and objects. I have unfolded to the view of the attentive reader what I *know* to be the motives and intentions of its instigators. I have, by this means, endeavored to undeceive the honest portion of that great American community, who have not had sufficient opportunities to penetrate the veil of their masked designs, and have been imposed upon by their false pretensions. The very acts of the insurgents—even the whole systematic course of their proceedings—prove clearly the correctness of my charges and expositions. It will be seen that, instead of a desire to establish and perpetuate the liberal institutions of freedom and equality of rights, they have taken up arms against the Mexican government from motives of personal aggrandizement, avaricious adventure, and unlimited, enduring oppression. The alarming fact is also clearly and fully substantiated, that the influence of the SLAVEHOLDING PARTY in the United States is now so completely in the ascendant, and so thoroughly sways the deliberations and proceedings of our Federal Government, that it makes it the passive, if not the active, instrument, in extending and permanently establishing that horrible system of oppression, even in regions where it had been destroyed by the power of moral virtue and republican principle.

The period has indeed arrived — THE CRISIS IS AT HAND—when the wise, the virtuous, the patriotic, the philanthropic of this nation, must examine, and reflect, and *deeply ponder* the momentous subject under consideration. Already we see the newspaper press in some of the free States openly advocating the system of slavery, with all its outrages and abominations.* Individuals occupying influential stations in the community at large, also countenance and encourage it, and even instigate the vile rabble to oppose, mal-treat, and trample on the necks of those who *dare* to plead the cause of the oppressed. At the ensuing session of our national Congress, the great battle will probably be fought, that must decide the question now at issue, and perhaps even *seal the fate of this Republic.* The Senators and Representatives of the people will then be called on to sanction the "independence of Texas," and also to provide for its admission, **as a SLAVEHOLDING STATE, into this Union.** These measures will positively be proposed, in case the Mexican Government fails to suppress the insurrection very soon, and to recover the actual possession of the territory. A few of our most eminent statesmen will resist the proposition with energy and zeal ; but unless the PUBLIC VOICE be raised against the unhallowed proceeding, and the sentiments of the people be most unequivocally expressed in the loudest tones of disapprobation, they will be unable to withstand the influence and power of their antagonists. Arouse then ! and let your voice be heard through your primary assemblies, your legislative halls, and the columns of the periodical press, in every section of your country.

Citizens of the United States !—Sons of the Pilgrims, and disciples of Wesley and Penn!—Coadjutors and pupils of Washington, Jefferson, and Franklin !—Advocates of Freedom, and the sacred "*Rights of Man !*"—Will you longer shut your eyes, and slumber in apathy, while the demon of oppression is thus stalking over the plains consecrated to the Genius of

* See two of the influential daily papers in New York —the Evening Star, and the Courier & Enquirer—with several others elsewhere,—approving of slavery in all its forms. These corrupt vehicles disseminate the most odious and tyrannical doctrines, in relation to the subject; and as a matter of course, they stand forth among the boldest champions, in advocating and encouraging the marauding crusade against Mexico.

Liberty and fertilized by the blood of her numerous martyrs?—Will you permit the authors of this gigantic project of national aggression, interminable slavery, and Heaven-daring injustice, to perfect their diabolical schemes through your supineness, or with the sanction of your acquiescence ? If they succeed in the accomplishment of their object, where will be your guarantee for the liberty which you, yourselves, enjoy ? When the advocates of slavery shall obtain the balance of power in this confederation ; when they shall have corrupted a few more of the aspirants to office among you, and opened an illimitable field for the operations of your heartless land-jobbers and slave-merchants, (to secure their influence in effecting the unholy purposes of their ambition,) how long will you be able to resist the encroachments of their tyrannical influence, or prevent them from usurping and exercising *authority* over you ? ARISE IN THE MAJESTY OF MORAL POWER, and place the seal of condemnation upon this flagrant violation of national laws, of human rights, and the eternal, immutable principles of Justice.

I will now present the reader with an extract from the celebrated speech of JOHN QUINCY ADAMS, delivered in the House of Representatives of the United States, May 25th, 1835. He takes some very important views of the subject before us, coinciding with, and also corroborating, much of what is here advanced. — Speaking of the constitutional powers of Congress, relative to the subject of slave emancipation, and supposing several cases that may be likely to occur, he proceeds as follows:—

" I suppose a more portentous case, certainly within the bounds of possibility—I would to God I could say not within the bounds of probability. You have been, if you are not now, at the very point of a war with Mexico—a war, I am sorry to say, so far as public rumor is credited, stimulated by provocations on our part from the very commencement of this Administration down to the recent authority given to General Gaines to invade the Mexican territory. It is said that one of the earliest acts of this Administration was a proposal made at a time when there was already much ill-humour in Mexico against the United States, that she should cede to the U. States a very large portion of her territory—large enough to constitute nine States equal in extent to Kentucky. It must be confessed that a device better calculated to produce jealousy, suspicion, ill-will, and hatred, could not have been contrived. It is further affirmed that this overture, offensive in itself, was made precisely at the time when a swarm of colonists from these United States were covering the Mexican border with land jobbing, and with slaves, introduced in defiance of the Mexican laws, by which slavery had been abolished throughout that Republic. The war now raging in Texas is a Mexican civil war, and a war for the re-establishment of slavery where it was abolished. It is not a servile war, but a war between slavery and emancipation, and every possible effort has been made to drive us into the war, on the side of slavery.

It is, indeed, a circumstance eminently fortunate for us that this monster, Santa Anna, has been de eated and taken,* though I cannot participate in that exquisite joy with which we have been told that every one having Anglo-Saxon blood in his veins must have been delighted on hearing that this ruffian has been shot, in cold blood, when a prisoner of war, by the Anglo-Saxon leader of the victorious Texian army Sir, I hope there is no member of this House, of other than Anglo-Saxon origin, who will deem it uncourteous that I, being myself in part Anglo-Saxon, must, of course, hold that far the best blood that ever circulated in human veins. Oh! yes sir! far be it from me to depreciate the glories of the Anglo-Saxon race; although there have been times when they bowed their necks and submitted to the law of conquest, beneath the ascendency of the Norman race But, sir, it has struck me as no inconsiderable evidence of the spirit which is spurring us into this war of aggression, of conquest, and of slave-making, that all the fires of ancient, hereditary national hatred are to be kindled, to familiarize us with the ferocious spirit of rejoicing at the massacre of prisoners in cold blood. Sir, is there not yet hatred enough between the races which compose your Southern population and the population of Mexico, their next neighbour, but you must go back eight hundred or a thousand years, and to another hemisphere, for the fountains of bitterness between you and them ? What is the temper of feeling between the component parts of your own Southern population, between your Anglo-Saxon, Norman French, and Moorish Spanish inhabitants of Louisiana, Mississippi, Arkansas, and Missouri ? between them all and the Indian savage, the original possessor of the land from which you are scourging him already back to the foot of the Rocky Mountains ? What between them all and the American negro, of African origin, whom they are holding in cruel bondage ? Are these elements of harmony, concord, and patriotism between the component parts of a nation starting upon a crusade of conquest? And what are the feelings of all this motly compound equally heterogeneous of the Mexican population ? Do not you, an Anglo-Saxon, slave-holding exterminator of Indians, from the bottom of your soul, hate the Mexican-Spaniard-Indian emancipator of slaves and abolisher of slavery ? And do you think your hatred is not with equal cordiality returned ? Go to the city of Mexico, ask any one of your fellow citizens who have been there for the last three or four years, whether they scarcely dare show their faces, as Anglo-Americans, in the streets Be assured, sir, that, however heartily you detest the Mexican, his bosom burns with an equally deep-seated detestation of you.

And this is the nation with which, at the instigation of your Executive Government, you are now rushing into war—into a war of conquest; commenced by aggression on your part, and for the re-establishment of slavery, where it has been abolished, throughout the Mexican Republic For your war will be with Mexico—with a Republic of twenty-four States, and a population of eight or nine millions of souls. It seems to be considered that this victory over twelve hundred men, with the capture of their commander, the President of the Mexican Republic, has already achieved the conquest of the whole Republic. That it may have achieved the independence of Texas, is not impossible. But Texas is to the Mexican Republic not more nor so much as the State of Michigan is to yours ;—that State of Michigan, the People of which are in vain claiming of you the performance of that sacred promise you made them, of admitting her as a State into the Union; that State of Michigan, which has greater grievances and heavier wrongs to allege against you for a decla-

* Mr. Adams, and many others, have been misled by false representations respecting Santa Anna's character.

ration of her independence, if she were disposed to declare it, than the People of Texas have for breaking off their union with the Republic of Mexico. Texas is an extreme boundary portion of the Republic of Mexico ; a wilderness only inhabited by the Indians until after the Revolution which separated Mexico from Spain; not sufficiently populous at the organization of the Mexican Confederacy to form a State by itself, and therefore united with Coahuila, where the greatest part of the indigenous part of the population reside. Sir, the history of all the emancipated Spanish American colonies has been, ever since their separation from Spain, a history of convulsionary wars ; of revolutions, accomplished by single and often very insignificant battles ; of chieftains, whose title to power has been the murder of their immediate predecessors. They have all partaken of the character of the first conquest of Mexico by Cortez, and of Peru by Pizarro ; and this, sir, makes me shudder at the thought of connecting our destinies indissolubly with theirs. It may be that a new revolution in Mexico will follow upon this captivity or death of their President and commanding general ; we have rumours, indeed, that such a revolution had happened even before his defeat; but I cannot yet see my way clear to the conclusion that either the independence of Texas, or the capture and military execution of Santa Anna, will save you from war with Mexico. Santa Anna was but one of a breed of which Spanish America for the last twenty-five years has been a teeming mother —soldiers of fortune, who, by the sword or the musket ball have risen to supreme power, and by the sword or the musket ball have fallen from it. That breed is not extinct; the very last intelligence from Peru tells of one who has fallen there as Yturbide, and Mina, and Guerrero, and Santa Anna have fallen in Mexico. The same soil which re-produced them is yet fertile to produce others. They produce themselves, with nothing but a change of the name and of the man Your war, sir, is to be a war of races—the Anglo-Saxon American pitted against the Moorish-Spanish-Mexican American; a war between the Northern and Southern halves of North America, from Passamaquoddy to Panama. Are you prepared for such a war ?

And again I ask, what will be your *cause* in such a war ? Aggression, conquest, and the re-establishment of slavery where it has been abolished. In that war, sir, the banners of *freedom* will be the banners of Mexico; and your banners, I blush to speak the word, will be the banners of slavery.

Sir, in considering these United States and the Mexican States as mere masses of power coming to collision against each other, I cannot doubt that Mexico will be the greatest sufferer by the shock. The conquest of all Mexico would seem to be no improbable result of the conflict, especially if the war should extend no farther than to the two mighty combatants. But will it be so confined ? Mexico is clearly the weakest of the two Powers, but she is not the least prepared for action. She has the more recent experience of war. She has the greatest number of veteran warriors; and although her highest chief has just suffered a fatal and ignominious defeat, yet that has happened often before to leaders of armies too confident of success and contemptuous of their enemy.—Even now, Mexico is better prepared for a war of invasion upon you than you are for a war of invasion upon her. There may be found a successor to Santa Anna, inflamed with the desire, not only of avenging her disaster, but what he and his nation will consider your perfidious hostility. The national spirit may go with him. He may not only turn the tables upon the Texian conquerors, but drive them for refuge within your borders, and pursue them into the heart of your own territories. Are you in a condition to resist him ? Is the success of your whole army, and all your veteran generals, and all your militia calls, and all your mutinous volunteers against a miserable band of five or six hundred invisible Seminole Indians, in your late campaign, an earnest of the energy and vigor with which you are ready to carry on that far otherwise formidable and complicated war?—complicated, did I say? And how complicated? Your Seminole war is already spreading to the Creeks, and. in their march of desolation, they sweep along with them your negro slaves, and put arms into their hands to make common cause with them against you, and how far will it spread, sir, should a Mexican invader, with the torch of liberty in his hand, and the standard of freedom floating over his head, proclaiming emancipation to the slave and revenge to the native Indian, as he goes, invade your soil? What will be the condition of your States of Louisiana, of Mississippi, of Alabama, of Arkansas, of Missouri, and of Georgia? Where will be your negroes? Where will be that combined and concentrated mass of Indian tribes, whom, by an inconsiderate policy, you have expelled from their widely distant habitations, to embody them within a small compass on the very borders of Mexico, as if on purpose to give the country a nation of natural allies in their hostilities against you? Sir, you have a Mexican, an Indian, and a negro war upon your hands, and you are plunging yourself into it blindfold; you are talking about acknowledging the independence of the Republic of Texas, and you are thirsting to annex Texas, aye, Coahuila, and Tamaulipas, and Santa Fe, from the source to the mouth of the Rio Bravo, to your already over-distended dominions. Five hundred thousand square miles of the territory of Mexico would not even now quench your burning thirst for aggrandizement.

But will your foreign war for this be with Mexico alone? No, sir. As the weaker party, Mexico, when the contest shall have once begun, will look abroad, as well as among your negroes and your Indians, for assistance. Neither Great Britain nor France will suffer you to make such a conquest from Mexico; no, nor even to annex the independent State of Texas to your Confederation, without their interposition. You will have an Anglo-Saxon intertwined with a Mexican war to wage. Great Britain may have no serious objection to the independence of Texas, and may be willing enough to take her under her protection, as a barrier both against Mexico and against you. But, as aggrandizement to you, she will not readily suffer it; and, above all, she will not suffer you to acquire it by conquest and the re-establishment of slavery. Urged on by the irresistible, overwhelming torrent of opinion, Great Britain has recently, at a cost of one hundred millions of dollars, which her People have joyfully paid, abolished slavery throughout all her colonies in the West Indies. After setting such an example, she will not—it is impossible that she should—stand by and witness a war for the re-establishment of slavery where it had been for years abolished, and situated thus in the immediate neighborhood of her islands. She will tell you, that if you must have Texas as a member of your Confederacy, it must be without the trammels of slavery, and if you will wage a war to handcuff and fetter your fellow-man, she will wage the war against you to break his chains. Sir, what a figure, in the eyes of mankind, would you make, in deadly conflict with Great Britain: she fighting the battles of emancipation, and you the battles of slavery; she the benefactress, and you the oppressor, of human kind! In such a war, the enthusiasm of emancipation, too, would unite vast numbers of her People in aid of the national rivalry, and all her natural jealousy against our aggrandizement. No war was ever so popular in England as that war would be against

slavery, the slave-trade, and the Anglo-Saxon descendant from her own loins

As to the annexation of Texas to your Confederation, for what do you want it? Are you not large and unwieldly enough already? Do not two millions of square miles cover surface enough for the insatiate rapacity of your land jobbers? I hope there are none of them within the sound of my voice. Have you not Indians enough to expel from the land of their fathers' sepulchres, and to exterminate? What, in a prudential and military point of view, would be the addition of Texas to your domain? It would be weakness, and not power. Is your southern and south-western frontier not sufficiently extensive? not sufficiently feeble? not sufficiently defenceless? Why are you adding regiment after regiment of dragoons to your standing army? Why are you struggling, by direction and by indirection, to raise *per saltum* that army from less than six to more than twenty thousand men? Your commanding General, now returning from his excursion to Florida, openly recommends the increase of your Army to that number. Sir, the extension of your sea coast frontier from the Sabine to the Rio Bravo would add to your weakness tenfold; for now it is only weakness with reference to Mexico. It would then be weakness with reference to Great Britain, to France, even perhaps to Russia, to every naval European Power, which might make a quarrel with us for the sake of settling a colony; but above all, to Great Britain. She, by her naval power, and by her American colonies, holds the keys of the gulf of Mexico. What would be the condition of your frontier from the mouth of the Mississippi to the mouth of the Rio del Norte, in the event of a war with Great Britain? Sir, the reasons of Mr. Monroe for accepting the Sabine as the boundary were three.—First, he had no confidence in the strength of our claim as far as the Rio Bravo; secondly, he thought it would make our union so heavy that it would break into fragments by its own weight; thirdly, he thought it would protrude a long line of sea coast, which, in our first war with Great Britain, she might take into her own possession, and which we should be able neither to defend nor recover. At that time there was no question of slavery or of abolition involved in the controversy. The country belonged to Spain; it was a wilderness, and slavery was the established law of the land. There was then no project for carving out nine States, to hold eighteen seats in the other wing of this capitol, in the triangle between the mouths and the sources of the Mississippi and Bravo rivers.—But what was our claim? Why it was that La Salle, having discovered the mouth of the Mississippi, and France having made a settlement at New Orleans, France had a right to one-half the sea coast from the mouth of the Mississippi to the next Spanish settlement, which was Vera Cruz. The mouth of the Rio Bravo was about half way from the Balize to Vera Cruz; and so as grantees, from France of Louisiana, we claimed the Rio del Norte, though the Spanish settlement of Santa Fe was at the head of that river. France, from whom we had received Louisiana, utterly disclaimed ever having even raised such a pretension. Still we made the best of the claim that we could, and finally yielded it for the Floridas, and for the line of the 42d degree of latitude from the source of the Arkansas river to the South sea. Such was our claim, and you may judge how much confidence Mr. Monroe could have in its validity. The great object and desire of the country then was to obtain the Floridas. It was Gen. Jackson's desire, and in that conference with me to which I have heretofore alluded, and which it is said he does not recollect, he said to me that so long as the Florida rivers were not in our possession, there could be no safety for our whole Southern country.

But, sir, suppose you should annex Texas to these United States, another year would not pass before you would have to engage in a war for the conquest of the Island of Cuba. What is now the condition of the Island?—Still under the nominal protection of Spain,—consuming her own vitals in a civil war for the succession of the crown. Do you expect, that whatever may be the issue of that war, she can retain even the nominal possession of Cuba? After having lost *all* her continental colonies in North and South America, Cuba will stand in need of more efficient protection: and above all, the protection of a naval power. Suppose that naval power should be Great Britain. There is Cuba at your very door; and if you spread yourself along a naked coast, from the Sabine to the Rio Bravo, what will be your relative position towards Great Britain, with not only Jamaica, but Cuba, and Porto Rico in her hands, and abolition for the motto to her union cross of St. George and St. Andrew? Mr. Chairman, do you think I am treading on fantastic grounds? Let me tell you a piece of history, not far remote. Sir, many years have not passed away since an internal revolution in Spain subjected that country and her king for a short time to the momentary government of the Cortes. That revolution was followed by another, by which, under the auspices of a French army with the Duke d'Angouleme at their head, Ferdinand the VII. was restored to a despotic throne; Cuba had followed the fortunes of the Cortes when they were crowned with victory; and when the counter revolution came, the inhabitants of the island, uncertain what was to be their destination, were for some time in great perplexity what to do for themselves. Two considerable parties arose in the island, one of which was for placing it under the protection of Great Britain, and another was for annexing it to the confederation of these United States. By one of these parties I have reason to believe that overtures were made to the Government of Great Britain. By the other *I know* that overtures were made to the Government of the United States. And I further know that secret, though irresponsible assurances were communicated to the then President of the United States, as coming from the French Government, that *they* were secretly informed that the British Government had determined to take possession of Cuba. Whether similar overtures were made to France herself, I do not undertake to say—but that Mr. George Canning, then the British Secretary of State for Foreign Affairs, was under no inconsiderable alarm, lest under the pupilage of the Duke d'Angouleme, Ferdinand the VII. might commit to the commander of a French naval squadron the custody of the Moro Castle, is a circumstance also well known to me. It happened that just about that time a French squadron of considerable force was fitted out, and received sailing orders for the West Indies, without formal communication of the fact to the British Government—and that as soon as it was made known to him, he gave orders to the British Ambassador at Paris to demand, in the most peremptory tone, what was the destination of that squadron, and a special and positive disclaimer that it was intended even to visit the Havana; and this was made the occasion of mutual explanations, by which Great Britain, France, and the United States, not by the formal solemnity of a treaty, but by the implied engagement of mutual assurances of intention, gave pledges of honor to each other, that neither of them should in the then condition of the island take it, or the Moro Castle, as its citadel, from the possession of Spain. This engagement was on all sides faithfully performed—but, without it, who doubts that from that day to this either of the three Powers might have taken the island and held it in undisputed possession?

At this time circumstances have changed—popular revolutions both in France and Great Britain have perhaps curbed the spirit of conquest in Great Britain, and France may have enough to do to govern her kingdom of Algiers. But Spain is again convulsed with a civil war for the succession to her crown; she has irretrievably lost all her colonies on both continents of America. It is impossible that she should hold much longer a shadow of dominion over the islands of Cuba and Porto Rico—nor can those islands, in their present condition, form independent nations, capable of protecting themselves. They must for ages remain at the mercy of Great Britain or of these United States, or of both; Great Britain is even now about to interfere in this war for the Spanish succession. If by the utter imbecility of the Mexican confederacy this revolt of Texas should lead immediately to its separation from that Republic, and its annexation to the United States, I believe it impossible that Great Britain should look on while this operation is performing with indifference. She will see that it must shake her own whole colonial power on this continent, in the Gulf of Mexico, and in the Carribbean seas, like an earthquake—she will see, too, that it endangers her own abolition of slavery in her own colonies. A war for the restoration of slavery where it has been abolished, if successful in Texas, must extend over all Mexico; and the example will threaten her with imminent danger of a war of colors in her own islands. She will take possession of Cuba and of Porto Rico, by cession from Spain or by the batteries from her wooden walls; and if you ask her by what authority she has done it, she will ask you, in return, by what authority you have extended your sea coast from the Sabine to the Rio Bravo. She will ask you a question more perplexing, namely—by what authority you, with freedom, independence, and democracy upon your lips, are waging a war of extermination to forge new manacles and fetters, instead of those which are falling from the hands and feet of man. She will carry emancipation and abolition with her in every fold of her flag—while your stars, as they increase in numbers, will be overcast with the murky vapors of oppression, and the only portion of your banners visible to the eye, will be the blood-stained stripes of the task master."

Since the present insurrection commenced, the excitement against our citizens in Mexico has risen, of course, to a higher pitch than ever. The foregoing speech delivered by Mr. Adams, and translated into the Spanish language, as before stated, was published in that country, with the following introductory remarks:—

" The discourse annexed, which was delivered in the House of Representatives of the United States, by the Ex-President, John Quincy Adams, is a Document which, in the actual state of things, ought to attract the attention of all reflecting men; not absolutely as a specimen of oratory, but as that of the effusions of a sublimated soul, which soars above the corruption of the times, dares to promulgate the truth in its purity, and plead in defence of the principles of Justice, so scandalously trampled upon in his country with respect to the question relating to Texas.

The speculators in Land, at New Orleans and New York, have conceived the project of enriching themselves, by wresting from Mexico the territory of Texas; and as it became requisite to give an air of honesty to their base intentions, they have, with a plausible pretext, fastened upon the much abused epithet of *Liberty.*—But there is another design, which threatens the political existence of the *Hispano-American Nations,*—especially of Central America,

and New Granada, which by their geographical
position, and peculiar advantages in the commercial
sphere, may be considered as the *Keys* of the Continent : this design is the establishment of SLAVERY.
So that, if the Anglo-Americans succeed in their effort
of appropriating Texas to themselves, Mexicans,
Central-Americans, Granadians, tremble for your
destiny ! because, on a day least thought of, you will
become the prey of the insatiable Anglo-Saxon-
American cupidity; and the soil on which you now
tread, will be sold by lots at each Public Exchange of
the United States, to fill the purses of your Invaders,
and to transfer your plantations and other territorial
possessions to the hands of the trafficking mob, who
look forward to the moment to subjugate you.

The discourse of Mr. Adams reveals important
mysteries—it discovers plans, which he magnani-
mously condemns, and publishes that which, afar off,
all cannot see. Mr. Adams, an Anglo-American,
well knows the character of his countrymen; and
guided by a pure zeal for the cause of humanity, and
of justice, he has not dreaded to draw upon himself
the hatred of his depraved cotemporaries, and at-least
to preserve his personal honor, since he cannot that
of his country, before the tribunal of mankind and of
posterity, by affording in this manner to Philanthropists, to the truly liberal, and to all worthy men, the
satisfaction of seeing him defend, with courage and
energy, the noble cause of the freedom of the human
race.

But above all, the Mexicans ought to know the
high destinies to which Providence calls them in the
New World, by confiding to their care nothing less
than the guardianship of this same Liberty. What
imports it, that hireling Editors and Land-jobbers
vociferate ? if the whole world is to be the witness
and judge of the rectitude of this noble cause ? What
imports it, that general Santa Anna has had a disas-
trous encounter, if his personal fate (however to be
lamented) be not that which led him on to battle ?
Is he the only Mexican who loves his country ? Is
he the sole champion of liberty, whom Mexico can
call forth to drive from the soil of the country the
Banditti who propose to domineer over a part of it,
in order forthwith to contaminate it by introducing
hordes of Negro Slaves ? This warfare admits of no
compromise: it must terminate either in the beneficent
triumph of the universal emancipation of the human
race, or else the sacrifice of all liberty throughout
America, by establishing slavery where it has been
abolished, or has not existed, through the instrumen-
tality of the degenerate portion of the English race,
which now inhabit that part of the United States
extending from the Capital to the boundaries of
Texas."

We have received accounts of some late
and very interesting proceedings in the British
Parliament, connected with the important
subject before us. These proceedings may
well attract the attention of those concerned
in the splendid *nefarious* project of converting
the Texas country into an immense SLAVE
MARKET for the freebooters of America and
Europe. The subject increases in importance,
as the eyes of the world are opening to the
enormity and iniquity of the scheme.

In the House of Commons, June 30th, the
subject of the "Revolt in Texas" was thus
introduced and discussed :—

Mr. B. Hoy said he was anxious to know from
the noble Lord, the Secretary of Foreign Affairs,
whether he had received any communication relative
to the establishment of slavery and the slave trade in
Texas.

Lord Palmerston observed that the inhabitants of
Texas were in a state of revolt against the Mexican
Government, and the result of that revolt was not
as yet decided. If the Mexican Government should
succeed, they would, of course, enforce their laws on
the inhabitants ; but if the contest should have
another result, and that there should be a separation
of Texas from the Mexican Government, and their
establishment as an independent power ensued, in
such case the laws of Mexico would not be applied.
He should, however, state, that no communication
could have taken place between Texas and the British
Government.

Mr. B. Hoy announced his intention of bringing
the subject under the consideration of Parliament.

Dr. Lushington wished to ask his noble friend a
question with reference to Texas. He was desirous
of knowing whether any information had been received of the importation of slaves from Texas into
the United States. Though he believed there was no
treaty between this country and the United States
which could compel them to put an end to such a
system, yet they were bound not to sanction a con-
tinuance of such a practice.

Lord Palmerston replied, that no such information
had been received by Government.

The London *Patriot*, of July 6th, copies the
remarks of John Quincy Adams in Congress,
from a New York paper, and makes ample
comments upon the subject in general. The
editor observes:—

The British public ought to be made aware of
what is going on at present in Texas ; of the true
cause and the true nature of the contest between
the Mexican authorities and the American slave
jobbers.

Texas has long been the Naboth's vineyard of
brother Jonathan. For twenty years or more, an
anxiety has been manifested to push back the boundary of the United States territory, of which the
Sabine river is the agreed line, so as to include the
rich alluvial lands of the Delta of the Colorado, at
the head of the Gulf of Mexico.—There are stronger
passions at work, however, than the mere lust of
territory—deeper interests at stake. Texas belongs
to a republic which has abolished slavery; the
object of the Americans is to convert it into a
slaveholding state ; not only to make it the field of
slave cultivation, and a market for the Maryland
slave trade, but by annexing it to the Federal Union,
to strengthen in Congress the preponderating influence of the southern slave-holding states.

This atrocious project is the real origin and cause
of the pretended contest for Texian Independence—
a war, on the part of the United States, of unpro-
voked aggression for the vilest of all purposes.

In alluding to the remarks of Mr. Adams; as
before mentioned, the same writer says :—

They ought to enlist the feelings of every British
philanthropist, every British Christian, in support
of the noble minded men who are standing forward
in the United States, to resist the torrent of national
iniquity. We call upon the country to raise its
voice. Trust not to the smooth words and slow
movements of Lord Palmerston. It will be seen
from our Parliamentary record, that on Thursday
night, the subject of what the papers call the *Revolt
in Texas* was mooted in the House of Commons.
In answer to the question, whether government had
received any communication relative to the *establishment of slavery and the slave trade in Texas*, Lord
Palmerston observed, that the inhabitants of Texas

were in revolt against the Mexican Government, and that, if they succeeded, in such case the laws of Mexico would not be applied. Was this a reply worthy of a British statesman? Mr. Hoy *announced his intention of bringing the subject under the consideration of Parliament ; and we will take* CARE THAT THE SUBJECT SHALL NOT BE STIFLED. Dr. Lushington asked, whether government had received any information of the *importation of slaves from Texas into the United States ?* Was the honorable and learned gentleman content with the answer he obtained? We are sure he was not.

At a subsequent meeting of Parliament, the following highly important proceedings are noticed in the London *Times* —Although the motion of Mr. Hoy was finally withdrawn, the great interest manifested upon the occasion, both by the mover and Mr. H. G. Ward, who seconded the motion, it may fairly be presumed that *the English abolitionists will not be disposed to let the question rest there.* No man in Europe is better acquainted with the subject than the gentleman last named. His long residence in Mexico, in the character of Envoy Extraordinary, gave him ample opportunity to acquire a thorough knowledge of political affairs, as well as the state of things generally:—and it will be seen that his testimony fully corroborates (as far as it goes) the statements of Mr. Adams, and likewise many of those in the preceding pages of this pamphlet. The observations of Lord Palmerston, though *ostensibly* calculated to neutralize the feelings of the other members, will have a directly contrary effect upon the people of England ; and according to his own admission, upon certain contingencies, (should "fresh circumstances" arise) the government would feel itself bound, or a least authorized, to look to the matter. In what light will it view the *invasion* of General Gaines, and the open, *unmolested* armament and marching of troops, from different parts of the United States, into the territory?

HOUSE OF COMMONS.—August 6.

TEXAS.

Mr. B. Hoy rose to bring forward the motion of which he had given notice. It was on a subject of the utmost importance to the cause of humanity, of immense importance to our colonial possessions and to our merchants who had embarked 70,000,000 dollars in Mexico. If the United States were suffered to wrest Texas from Mexico, would not Cuba and other Mexican possessions fall a prey to the United States? The war now going on in Texas was a war not for independence, but for slavery ; and he would contend that should the revolt in Texas be successful, that province would still be bound by the treaty Mexico entered into with this country, when Texas formed part of the Mexican dominions, to prevent the carrying on of the slave trade within its territory ; the number of States in the Union had originally been 13 ; they were now increased to 26, and if Texas were added to the Union there could be no doubt the basis of the connection would be to establish slavery and the slave trade permanently in that province. He begged to ask the noble Lord opposite, Lord Palmerston, if, within the last ten days, he had not received an application from the Mexican Government for the good offices of this country

to remonstrate with the United States against the gross violation of Treaties, and the aggressions of their southern states.—The honorable member read extracts from speeches of Mr. Huskisson and Mr. John Q. Adams, to show the importance to America in a commercial point of view, of annexing Texas to its territory.

It is now for this house to consider whether, after the enormous sums expended in abolishing and putting down slavery it would render the whole of that expenditure useless, and to allow slavery to take deep root in situations with respect to which this country had both the power and right of interference in suppressing it. But, supposing the independence of Texas to be established, and that it united itself to the United States, let the house consider what considerable commercial advantages the latter would gain over this country. By that junction, the United States would be brought within six weeks sail of China. Neither ought the importance of the possessions of the mining districts by America be lost sight of by this country. Those mines were of immense value—one alone having produced 30,000,000 dollars. Unless Mexico was assisted, as she ought to be, by this country, she would be so weakened as soon to become an easy victim to the ambition of the United States of America. The motion with which he intended to conclude was, for an address to the Crown to take such measures as were proper for the fulfilment of the existing treaty, by which this country was bound to co-operate with Mexico. He was of opinion that England ought not only to remonstrate with America, but to have a naval force on the coast to support Mexico against American aggressions.

The Hon. member concluded by moving : "That an humble address be presented to the Crown, praying that his Majesty will be graciously pleased to direct that such measures be taken as to his Majesty may seem proper, to secure the fulfilment of the existing treaty between this country and Mexico, and to prevent the establishment of slavery and traffic in slaves, in the province of Texas, in the Mexican territory."

Mr. H. G. Ward seconded the amendment, which involved a subject upon which he had been long and was deeply interested. The importance of Texas was but little known in this house or by the country. The province itself consisted of a large tract of the finest land, it had numerous good and only two bad ports, and the possession of it would give to the parties obtaining it the full command of the whole gulf of Mexico. The Mexican Government on its first intercourse with this country, an intercourse of increased and still increasing commercial importance to this country, had stipulated for the abolition in its territory of the slave trade, and he (Mr. Ward) could state that this stipulation had been most rigidly enforced and observed ; and he did not believe that there were now in the Mexican states, except Texas, 20 slaves. To Texas the United States had long turned covetous eyes, and to obtain possession of that province had been the first object of its policy. During his residence in Mexico, America contrived to have a proposal made to the Mexican Government, offering 10,000,000 dollars for certain privileges in Texas, and that proposition having been refused, America then proceeded to encourage the settlement of Texas of the refuse of her own southern states, who took possession of the land without title or pretension to any title, and thus drew into it a population exclusively slave and American. A declaration of independence next followed. That declaration issued from men recognizing no law, and signed by only one Mexican, the President of the Province, a man of talent, it was true, but who had dealt most largely in Texas lands, and sougdt his own advantage. He was supposed to have formed a connexion with some influential men of the American Cabinet and amongst them with Mr. Forsyth. What then had followed?—America having created a population in Texas in the way he had stated, and having given to it every possible assistance, a committee of foreign relations in the Senate, came in with a report signed by Mr. Clay, for whom he entertained a high respect, discussing the necessity of recognizing the declaration of the independence of Texas. The tendency of the whole report was to show the propriety, at a future time, to annex Texas to the United States. The question therefore, for the House to consider was—first, the general policy of allowing a state, without remonstrance, to extend itself, and thus put an end to the trade between this country and Mexico—the connexion between which could be completely cut off by a few American privateers ensconced in the Texian ports. The principle had been disclaimed in 1835, when it was proposed to annex part of Cuba to the United States, and that instance ought to guide this country in not allowing this contemplated extension of the American territory. The next consideration was, whether the country would now allow a renewal and an increase of the slave trade? Such would be the result of this policy on the part of America, and from a pamphlet he had received this day, it appeared that the non-slavery states of America had themselves been roused to a sense of their own danger if that policy were successful. It was well known that there had long been a struggle between the slave states and non-slave states in Congress, and parties were equally balanced; but if Texas should eventually be annexed to the Federal Union, 18 votes in Congress at large of that most degrading feature in the civilized world—slavery On all these grounds, he most cordially supported the motion of the honorable member from Southampton. (Hear, hear.)

Lord Palmerston observed, that if it at the beginning of the observations he should have to make to the house, he said that he did not feel himself at liberty to agree to the proposal of the honorable member for Southampton, he trusted that neither the honorable member nor the house would imagine that it was a proof that he did not feel the importance of its object, or that his Majesty's Government were not as much animated as was the honorable member, with the desire to put an end to the evils to which the address he had moved so mainly related. (Hear, hear.) He [Lord Palmerston] trusted that he should be able to prove to the house that the address moved for was at present, in some respects, unnecessary, and in other respects premature. The observations of the two honorable gentlemen who had preceded him, divided themselves into two different branches—the one relating to the political part of the question, and the other relating to the trade in slaves.

With regard to the political question, undoubtedly the possibility that the province of Texas might be added to the United States, was a subject which ought seriously to engage the attention of the House and of the country, but he did not think that the events which had occurred afforded any ground for supposing that there was any such probability of its occurring to call upon this house to address the Crown with reference to that matter. The state of Texas at present was this—a revolt had taken place there; the Mexican army had been despatched for the purpose of putting it down. The first operations had been greatly successful, but a part of the army

having considerably advanced before the rest, it was surprised by the Texian force, routed with great slaughter, and the President taken prisoner. It might be possible that the resistance of the people of Texas might prevail against the authorities of Mexico, but, on the other hand, the numerical strength lay with the army of the Mexican Government, who, from the last accounts that were received, were preparing to make fresh efforts to reinforce their army, and from what had already happened the final result of the struggle could not be inferred.

With respect to the conduct of the United States of America in the matter, although he was aware that individuals in those States had given great assistance to the revolting population of Texas, yet the conduct of the responsible Government of America was the reverse. If regard were had to the President's Message to Congress, it would be found to contain an unequivocal declaration of that Government to take no part in the Mexican civil war, and that in accordance with that declaration, orders had been issued to enforce the laws in the prevention of individuals mixing themselves up in the matter. He [Lord Palmerston] had that opinion of the honor and good faith of the Government of America, as not to suppose that they would not act up to that declaration; and he thought fresh circumstances ought to arise before an address should be sent to the Crown on the political branch of the question. (Hear, hear.)

Now, with regard to that part of the question which related to the trade in slaves, the honorable gentleman opposite had remarked that no correspondence had been laid before the House with regard to the progress or diminution of the slave trade, supposed to exist in Texas, while other places were given. The fact was so; and the explanation he had to offer was, that his Majesty's Government had no agent in the province of Texas, and they had only lately received information from the British Minister at Mexico, bearing on the illicit trade in slaves supposed to be carried on in Texas. It would be a greater evil, much to be deplored, if the course of the civil war were to lead to an extension or re-establishment of slavery. That was a matter deserving the attention of the house; and if the house supposed that his Majesty's Government were either indifferent or unwilling to bestow the most vigilant care to prevent such an evil he should be willing to agree in thinking with the honorable member from Southampton it fitting to admonish the Government in the manner he proposed; but he [Lord Palmerston] assured the house the Government required no such stimulus to perform their duty, and he thought that what they were now doing might be accepted as a proof that they were anxious and active in endeavoring to put down the slave trade in every part of the world, and to prevent its springing up in quarters where it did not already exist; but he did not think there was any considerable danger of such an evil being the result of the Mexican civil war, for it was evident that either Texas must be conquered and yield to the Mexican authority or that it, by succeeding in its struggle would become an independent state; or thirdly, add itself to the United States of America. Now, if the Mexican authority were re-established, no more encouragement to the slave trade would be given in Texas than other Mexican states. Again, if the Mexican authority was thrown off, and the independence of Texas declared, it would then be open to this country to interfere and put down any trade in slaves that might be carried on.—Lastly, if Texas should, in the progress of events, become a member of the United States of America, thought slaves might be sent there from other states, there would be no real danger of the importation of slaves from the coast of Africa, or the islands of the West Indies. He was inclined to believe that an importation into Texas of slaves from Cuba had taken place, but he had not heard of any such importation from the coast of Africa. With regard to the importation of slaves from Cuba, he must say, that it had occured before the treaty concluded between Spain and this country, for suppressing the slave trade, had come into operation. The statement of the honorable member for Southampton, therefore, applied to a time antecedent to the ratification of the treaty.

The noble Lord then entered into various particulars of the measures taken by the Government with foreign powers for the suppression of the slave trade, and added, if the Government should receive any authentic accounts of the introduction of slaves in Texas, it would be their wish as well as duty, to take such immediate steps as would put it down. Now, as to the political question he thought there were no grounds whatever why this government should interfere politically. As to that part of the address which called on the crown to interfere to prevent the traffic in slaves in Texas, he thought it would involve a censure on the Government they had did not deserve, considering the measures they had already adopted, and on these grounds he must oppose the motion.

Dr. Lushington said there were several circumstances under which this country possessed a right to interfere to prevent the traffic in slaves in Texas. So long as Texas remained in a state of dependency on Mexico, or did not establish its independence, this country had a right to insist on its observation of the treaty which we had made with Mexico, of which, under such circumstances, it must be considered as still forming a part. If it did establish its independence, we could recognise it as a state on such conditions as we pleased, and could make the abolition of the slave trade one of them. But if the state was received into the union of the North American states, then we could demand that it should be bound by the treaties which we had contracted with the government of those states.

Dr. Bowring thought we were bound to *remonstrate with the Government of North America against the introduction of any slave-dealing state into the Union.*

Mr. F. Buxton expressed his belief that if the Americans should obtain possession of Texas, which had been truly described as forming one of the fairest harbors in the world, a greater impulse would be given to the slave trade than had been experienced for many years. If the British Government did not interfere to prevent the Texian territory from falling into the hands of the American slave holders, in all probability a greater traffic in slaves would be carried on during the next 50 years that had ever before existed. The war at present being waged in Texas, differed from any war which had ever been heard of.

It was not a war for the extension of territory—it was not a war of aggression—it was not one undertaken for the advancement of national glory; it was a war which had for its sole object the obtaining of a market for slaves.—(Hear, hear.) He would not say that the American Government connived at the proceedings which had taken place; but it was notorious that the Texians had been supplied with munitions of war of all sorts by the slave holders of the United States—(hear, hear.) Without meaning to cast any censure upon the Government, he thought the House had a right to demand that the Secretary

for foreign affairs adopt strong measures to prevent the establishment of a new and more extensive market for the slave trade than had ever before existed. The noble Lord ought immediately to open negociations on this subject, not only with the Mexican, but with the United States Government, which latter had always professed to be anxious for the extinction of the slave trade.

After a few words from Mr. Hume, Sir F. French and Sir J. R. Reid, in condemnation of the proceeding of the Texians, the amendment was withdrawn.

It is clearly evident that neither of the speakers, here quoted, were *fully* aware of the extent to which the United States government has lent its sanction to this diabolical crusade. It may be presumed, however, that they will learn it in due time.—And it is manifest that (according to the sentiments here expressed by them) they cannot stand by and look coldly on, while the process of usurpation and aggression are perfecting their work, if they do but thoroughly understand it.

Since the preceding pages were first prepared for the press, I have, in pursuing the investigation of this highly important subject, noted the principal incidents connected with it, as they have been unfolded to view in the progress of events. In treating upon it further, I shall proceed in a somewhat more desultory manner, touching upon the different topics and occurrences in the order of time suited to the general purpose.

Such were the open, glaring violations of laws and treaties, by the marauding brigands in the South and West ; so completely *blinded* or *corrupted* were the great majorities of the people in the regions bordering on Texas ; and so totally apathetic were the officers of the United States government,—or so thoroughly had they identified their feelings, their interests, and their actions, with the insurgents,—that some of our most patriotic and law abiding citizens became alarmed, both for the honor and peace of this nation. The following very interesting notice was taken of certain proceedings in Cincinnati, Ohio, in the summer of 1836, by *Charles Hammond, Esq.,* one of the ablest Lawyers in America:—

From the Cincinnati Daily Gazette.

"PROSECUTOR READ AND TEXAS."

We published yesterday, without comment, a communication from N. C. Read, Esq., on matters and things connected with Texas. Mr. Read has devoted himself very considerably for the last eight or ten months, to Texan affairs He has speechified often and again—has concocted resolutions, and has got up meetings to adopt them, and has otherwise been active in procuring that to be done, which has been effected, in aid of Texas, in this vicinity. In noticing certain proceedings in Fulton, in Monday's Gazette, the presence of Mr. Read was mentioned, not for the purpose of singling him out for distinction, but simply to note the extraordinary fact, that the Prosecuting Attorney should make himself conspicuous in denouncing the law of the land, and declaring a determination to disregard it. This fact occurred to me as evidencing too much of the prevalent spirit, to substitute the present dispositions of a supposed majority, right or wrong, for the established and permanent laws of the country: a spirit, which I apprehend, ever has been the great active agent in subverting regular governments, in every age of the world. Nothing in Mr. Read's communication changes my views of the subject.

Since early last winter, a series of transactions have passed before us, in open day, the undisguised object of which has been to enlist troops and procure arms to aid the Texans in their war with Mexico. Troops have been enlisted—arms have been obtained. Their military parades have been exhibited in our streets, they have embarked at our wharf, have proceeded to Texas, united themselves with her troops, and joined with them in battle against Mexico. In affecting all this many individuals have taken a predominant part. Public speaking has been one mode of operating upon the citizens, and when it so operates as to induce action, the speaker and the actor become associated, in the consequences of the act, whether for commendation or crime.

Am I not correct, when I say men and arms, for military purposes, have been furnished here? Has it not been boasted that the cannon used at San Jacinto, was supplied by Cincinnati? Is it not a fact, that every stand of public arms deposited at this place, by the state, have been sent to Texas, with the connivance of those who had charge of them? And can any man seriously suppose that the real character of these doings can be changed, by calling the men ' *emigrants,*' and the arms '*hollow ware?*' Associated pickpockets and burglars substitute cant phrases for thief and robber; and yet, Mr. Read, as Prosecuting Attorney, would laugh at a defence predicated upon such definitions. Who would not? and what is the distinction between the cases?

Is it an offence against any known law, thus to furnish men and arms to aid Texas in her war with Mexico? Let Texas and Mexico be regarded as equally independent States, engaged in war with each other, the United States is neutral in this war. As a neutral, what are her duties, as one of the community of nations. Independent of the law of Congress, which will be given in its place, the law of nations defines the duty of the United States in her present position. What this law of nations requires, is thus pointed out by Mr. Jefferson, when Secretary of State, in a letter to the French Minister Genet, of date June 17, 1793:

" You think, sir, that this opinion is also contrary to the law of nature, and the usages of nations. We are of opinion that it is dictated by that law and usage; and this had been very maturely inquired into, before it was adopted as a principle of conduct. But we will not assume the exclusive right of saying what that law and usage is. Let us appeal to enlightened and disinterested judges. None is more so than Vattel. He says, 1. 3, s. 104, 'as long as a neuter nation wishes to enjoy this situation with certainty, it ought to show, in every thing, an exact impartiality between those who are at war. For if it favored the one, to the prejudice of the other, it cannot complain when that other shall treat it as an adherent and associate of its enemy. Its neutrality would be a fraudulent one, of which none would be the dupe. Let us see then wherein consists that impartiality which a neutral people ought to observe.

" It regards war only, and comprehends two things. 1st. To give no succour when not obliged thereto; not to furnish, freely, either troops, arms, ammunition, or any thing which directly serves for war. I say, *to give no succour, and not to give it equally;* for it would be absurd in a state to succour two enemies at the same time. And besides, it would be impossible to do it with equality; the same things, the same

number of troops, the same quantity of arms, ammunition, &c. furnished in different circumstances, are no longer equivalent succours.' If the neutral power may not, consistent with its neutrality, furnish men to either party, for their aid in war, as little can either enrol them in the neutral territory, by the law of nations. Wolf, s. 1174, says, 'Since a right of raising soldiers is a right of majesty, which cannot be violated by a foreign nation, it is not permitted to raise soldiers on the territory of another, without the consent of its sovereign.' And Vattel, before cited, 1. 3, s. 15, 'The right of raising soldiers belonging only to the nation, or its sovereign, no one can enrol them in a foreign country, without the permission of the sovereign. Those who undertake to engage soldiers in a foreign country without permission of the sovereign—and in general whomsoever corrupts the subjects of others, violates one of the most sacred rights of the prince and of the nation. It is the crime which is called *plagiat* or man-theft. There is no political state which does not severely punish it.' For I choose to refer you to the passage, rather than follow it through all its developements. The testimony of these and other writers on the law and usage of nations, with your own just reflections on them, will satisfy you that the United States, in prohibiting all the belligerent powers from equipping, arming and manning vessels of war, in their ports, have exercised a right and a duty with justice, with great moderation. By our treaties with several of the belligerent powers, which are a part of the laws of our land, we have established a state of peace with them —But without appealing to treaties, we are at peace with them all, by the laws of nature, for, by nature's law, man is at peace with man, till some aggression is committed, which, by the same law authorizes one to destroy another, as his enemy. For our citizens, then, to *commit murders* and depredations on the members of nations at peace with us, or to combine to do it, appeared to the executive, and to those whom they consulted, as much against the laws of the land as *to murder or rob, or combine to murder or rob,* its own citizens—and as much to require punishment, as if done within their limits, or on the high seas, where they have a territorial jurisdiction, that is to say, one which reaches their own citizens only —this being an appropriate part of each nation on an element where all have a common jurisdiction. So say our laws as we understand them ourselves."

[State Papers, vol. 1, p. 91, &c.]

According to the law as laid down by Mr. Jefferson, the Texas movements in Cincinnati, are no better than combinations to *murder and rob.* Does this jar upon the feelings of Mr. Read and others who have acted with him? Let them recollect from whence and from whom the definition comes:—it is not mere editorial vituperation. Congress, however, has not treated these doings as of a grade of crime equal to robbery or murder—it has constituted them misdemeanors. The act of April 20, 1818, sections one, two, and six, provides:

1. *Be it enacted, &c.* That if any citizen of the United States shall, within the territory or jurisdiction thereof, accept and exercise a commission to serve a foreign prince, state, colony, district, or people, in war, by land or by sea, against any prince, state, colony, district, or people, with whom the United States are at peace, the person so offending shall be deemed guilty of a high misdemeanor, and shall be fined not more than two thousand dollars, and shall be imprisoned not exceeding three years.

2. That if any person shall, within the territory or jurisdiction of the United States, enlist or enter himself, or hire or retain another person to enlist or enter himself, or to go beyond the limits or jurisdiction of the United States with intent to be enlisted or entered in the service of any foreign prince, state,

colony, district, or people, as a soldier, or as a marine or seaman, on board of any vessel of war, letter of marque, or privateer, every person, so offending, shall be deemed guilty of a high misdemeanor, and shall be fined not exceeding one thousand dollars, and be imprisoned not exceeding three years.

6. That if any person shall, within the territory or jurisdiction of the United States, begin or set on foot, or provide or prepare the means for, any military expedition or enterprise, to be carried on from thence against the territory or dominions of any foreign prince or state, or of any colony, district, or people, with whom the United States are [at] peace, every person, so offending, shall be deemed guilty of a high misdemeanor, and shall be fined, not exceeding three thousand dollars, and imprisoned not more than three years.

The resolution, of which Mr. Read avows the authorship, declares a determination not to obey this law, but to nullify it. Is this allowable in any citizen? Hear what Judge Paterson says upon this head, in the case of Wm. S. Smith, speaking in reference to a section of the then existing law, in the same terms as the 6th section above quoted.

"'The section which prohibits military enterprises against nations with which the United States are at peace, imparts no dispensing power to the President. Does the constitution give it? Far from it; for it explicitly directs, that he shall "take care that the laws be faithfully executed." This instrument, which measures out the powers, and defines the duties of the President, does not vest in him any authority to set on foot a military expedition against a nation with which the United States are at peace. And if a private individual, even with the knowledge and approbation of this high and pre-eminent officer of our government, should set on foot such a military expedition, how can he expect to be exonerated from the obligation of the law? Who holds the power of dispensation?—True, a *nolle prosequi* may be entered, a pardon may be granted; but these presume criminality, presume guilt, presume amenability, to judicial investigation and punishment, which are very different from a power to dispense with the law. Suppose, then, that every syllable of the affidavit is true, of what avail can it be on the present occasion? Of what use or benefit can it be to the defendant in a court of law? Does it speak by way of justification? The President of the United States cannot control the statute, nor dispense with its execution, and still less can he authorize a person to do what the law forbids. If he could, it would render the execution of the laws dependent on his will and pleasure, which is a doctrine that has not been set up, and will not meet with any supporters in our government. In this particular the law is paramount. Who has dominion over it? None but the legislature; and even they are not without their limitation in our republic. Will it be pretended, that the President could rightfully grant a dispensation and license to any of our citizens to carry on a war against a nation with whom the United States are at peace? Ingenious and learned counsel may imagine and put a number of cases in the wide field of conjecture; but we are to take facts as we find them, and to argue from the existing state of things at the time. If we were at war with Spain, there is an end to the indictment; but, if at peace, what individual could lawfully make war, or carry on a military expedition against the dominions of his Catholic majesty?" Smith & Ogden, 83, &c.

Here is the law of nations, the law of Congress, and the judicial opinion of a most eminent judge of the U. S. Supreme Court. All concur, in regarding as criminal, the doings that have passed before us for some time by-gone, in regard to Texas. A very plain proposition is involved. Have military supplies,

arms and ammunition been procured, for Texas, in Cincinnati? If they have, then has the law been violated—then are the individuals concerned obnoxious to legal punishment.

In the report of the doings of the identical Fulton Texas meeting, about which Mr. Read has written his communication, we find the following:

'The meeting was then addressed by N. C. Read and Captain Lawrence.'

Again:

'It was moved and seconded, That a committee of five be appointed to assist Capt. Lawrence in raising recruits and funds for the cause of Texas, which being put to vote, the following gentlemen were elected,—

'B. Hazen, L. Fagin, A. Gordon, E. Townsend, and E. Anderson.'

Now, this very self same Capt. Lawrence has opened and advertised a rendezvous, on Front street, for engaging emigrants; in other words, enlisting recruits. He proclaims that he acts under a Captain's commission from Texas. Mr. Read acts in concert with him, in declaring,

"That no law, either human or divine, except such as are formed by tyrants and for their sole benefit, forbids our assisting the Texians; and such law, if any exists, we do not as Americans choose to obey."

And this, in direct contradiction to the public and statute law above published, Mr. Read represents as merely using the liberty of speech!! Mr. Read's speeches and the acts of Captain Lawrence, go hand in hand. It is an insult to common sense to assume, that so gross a violation of law can be evaded upon the grounds put forth by Mr Read.

I have nothing to say to the *rhodomontade* in which Mr. Read has dealt so largely. It may go for what it is worth. My business is with palpable facts and existing laws. I would, however, remark, in conclusion, that no appeal has yet been made to Cincinnati for aid to the suffering women, children, and decrepid old men of Texas, exposed by war to the most horrible calamities. Our sympathies have been invoked for soldiers and munitions of war.—Let Mr. Read confine himself to these subjects.—When he makes an appeal in behalf of suffering humanity, in the form of bread and covering, then he may talk about it. No law forbids supplying these to an enemy. Mr. Read's appeals have been for the tented field, and that is quite a different case.

I have called our Texian patriots ' land brawlers.' I cannot take it back. Has not a whole Kentucky corps come home in dudgeon, because of some difficulty about land? Are not the Texians themselves disputing to the knife upon the same subject?—And why do our patriot volunteers prefer to be soldiers in Texas to soldiers at home, in defence of our own citizens, beleagured by a savage foe? It is land!— speculation! Any thing, rather than a generous disinterested love of the liberty that good government and wise laws secure and make permanent."

I have before adverted to the fact, that General Gaines, commander in chief of the army for the southern department of the United States, was authorized by the government to cross the boundary line—but I have *merely* adverted to it,—and as a matter of great importance in elucidating the views and designs of those in authority, as well as in showing the impression which it was calculated to make upon the minds of the Mexicans, and disinterested persons everywhere, I will ask the further attention of the reader to that particular topic. It may be presumed, that all are familiar with the *arguments* used by our government in its justification, upon that occasion. The documents, &c. which I shall quote, will give a full explanation, however, of the whole matter.

Notwithstanding the assumption, that a necessity existed for the United States' troops to take a position on the Sabine, or beyond it, *for the purpose of keeping the Indians in check*, it was known to all intelligent persons there, at the time, that the array of force thus called for was intended to encourage the insurgents in Texas. A letter from an officer in the United States army, published in the *Army and Navy Chronicle*, candidly admits this, and says of the advance of Gaines' troops to Nacogdoches:—

" It is to create the impression in Texas and Mexico, that the government of the United States takes a part in the controversy. It is in fact lending to the cause of Texas all the aid which it can derive from the countenance and apparent support of the United States, besides placing our troops in a situation to take an actual part in aid of the Texians, in case a reverse of their affairs should render aid necessary. The pretext of the anticipated invasion from the Indians in that quarter is unsupported by the least probable testimony, although Gen. Houston has issued a proclamation, dated at Nacogdoches, ordering out a body of 200 Texian militia 'to sustain the United States force at this place, until reinforcements can arrive from Gen. Gaines.' "

The very circumstance, that such a " proclamation" was issued by the insurgent Chief, shows what *connexion* there was in the arrangements of the United States and bandit forces. A part of the former had arrived at Nacogdoches, and a speedy junction was desirable, as the Mexicans (then victorious) were expected to press onward immediately, in overpowering numbers.

But the following extract of a letter, from a highly respectable gentleman residing at Nacogdoches, to the editor of the New York *Commercial Advertiser*, presents a truly graphic delineation of the actual state of things at that period. This letter is well authenticated; and, indeed, it has been fully corroborated by subsequent testimony. Americans! Read and reflect.—

"I am myself an American, and unless Providence has deprived me of those sympathies that prompt others, am as much disposed to love my countrymen, to feel for them, admire them, and to cherish our noble constitution and laws, as any other man; yet I have never been able to approve the Texan cause, and still less can I approve of the second fiddle game now playing here by one of the general officers of the United States army.

I came to Texas some seven years since, possessed, as I thought, of good titles to a league of land, purchased in New York of an individual who, to my certain knowledge, had sold many other leagues, and on my arrival, immediately applied to the proper officer to be put in possession of my land, when, much to my surprise, I was told that my titles were good for nothing; but was informed at the same time that I was welcome to land, and that I might select any vacant land, for which I should receive titles on conditions then enumerated, and which I thought but fair and equitable. I accordingly pos-

sessed myself of a league of fine land, took the oath of allegiance to Mexico, and have lived in prosperity and happiness till the Texan Revolution; since which time, I must confess, I have tasted more bitterness, grief and trouble, than I had done in all my past life before. The like declarations will be made by every American who settled in Texas, whenever they can do so without the fears that make them mute. I now allude to those Americans who had been settlers for any time. and who had fulfilled the conditions entitling them to their lands; and not to those who came for the express purpose of sowing a rebellion, organized and matured by those who had forged, or had purchased forged titles to lands, and were in advance, determined to create rebellion, that they might perfect those titles, if possible.

There came to Nacogdoches, about three years ago, a Mexican, named Almonte, who publicly informed the people that he had been sent by the government to see and enquire as to the then condition of Texas—that the Mexican government was displeased and humiliated to find that immense forgeries had been effected in land titles—which spurious titles were selling in every large city of the United States to the great deception and ruin of innocent individuals who purchased them—that complaints from American citizens had reached the government of Mexico, alleging fraud, not only in the speculators who sold these titles, but even in the Mexican authorities themselves; and that this practice must cease, or the government would feel constrained to act in such a manner as would convince the world of their disapprobation of such practices. Mr. Almonte further explained what titles were good, and what were bad; and it is worthy of remark, that those whose titles are worthless, have hated the man ever since, and were very anxious to have him shot, when he was lately taken with Santa Anna, on the score of his having been a spy among them three years before. Do not laugh, Messrs. Editors, at the idea of a man's being a spy within his own country, and by the orders of his own government.

Soon after came General Houston, late governor, late Cherokee, &c. &c., and later still from Washington, with, as he said, (both in the United States and here,) the private views of General Jackson in relation to Texas. General Houston told his friends in general, that his purpose was to revolutionize the country. Next came General Mason, agent for the New York company. Upon the meeting of these two *big bugs*, a discussion took place as to the proposed revolution, Houston for it, Mason at that time against it; the gentlemen waxed warm in the argument, and separated mutually displeased with each other. Mason going through to Mexico, and, as it is *asserted by Mexicans*, being the first man who conveyed the news of the proposed rebellion in Texas, to Mexico.

Next in turn was the change in the government effected by Santa Anna; and next the Texian Revolution. Was it not laughable to see these Texians, all of them, generally speaking, slave-holders, adhering to the constitution of 1824, one article of which emancipates all the slaves in Mexico! Was it not laughable to see them proclaiming a constitution, of which, eleven years ago, the Americans in Texas had prohibited the proclamation by Mexican authorities there, under the heaviest threats!—What man of common sense can believe in this *humbug?* None, gentlemen; none but those that have risked their thousands in this country; and they, whoever they may be, feign to believe it. The statements made throughout the United States, of tyranny and oppression on the part of Mexico toward the American citizens in Texas, are slanderous falsehoods, fabricated to create and nurture the worst prejudices and jealousies The Americans in Texas have had their own way in every case, and on every occasion; and whenever there happened a legislative act that was, from any cause, repugnant to the feelings of the people in Texas, it was silenced at once. In short, if there has existed a good cause of complaint in Texas, it was that men were too much their own masters, and too little under the restraint of any law. Any allegation to the effect that the Mexican government had deceived citizens of the United States in relation to promises of lands first made to them, is false, and I defy any one to show a forfeiture of titles to lands, *when the conditions of the grants had been fulfilled by the settler.*

Now, sir, as to the war: here I will ask Americans, (except the speculators,) how many military incursions, insurrections and rebellions, avowedly for the purpose of snatching Texas from its proper owners, will, in their mind, justify Mexico in driving from its territories the pirates that would thus possess themselves of the country? Be it remembered that those revolutions have never been attempted by the resident citizens of Texas, but in every case by men organized in the United States for the purpose, and coming from afar; why, a single provocation of this nature were ample justification; but Texas has, from the time of the adjustment of the boundary by Wilkinson and Farrara, experienced seven or eight. Now what is Mexico to do? Can it be expected that she will maintain a large army in Texas merely for the purpose of guarding against the attempts of a few? Certainly not. Were the population of the United States one of savages, from one of which we should not expect good policy, and that international equity which has heretofore been the boast of Americans, it might perhaps be expected; but Mexico has rested under the belief that when a few marauders should interfere with her possessions, the American people would not object to see them properly chastised. But, gentlemen, what at present seems to be the situation of affairs? Not only has Houston avowed that his acts were prompted by the highest authority within the United States, but a general officer of the army of the United States presents himself, with forces, upon the Mexican frontier. His first orders are to preserve perfect neutrality; and his particular attention is called to one of the articles of the treaty between the United States and Mexico, by which the contracting parties bind themselves to restrain their respective Indians, within their own limits. General Gaines having arrived, is at once in correspondence with the Texan officers, and despatches to Washington "information derived from the highest authority in Texas"—this, too, against the most positive information given to General Gaines, by respectable and intelligent people, that misrepresentations of all kinds were fabricating, and would be invented to induce him to cross. Upon the information thus given at Washington, by General Gaines, Mr. Secretary Cass writes that he has laid before the executive his letter, and that his construction, in the uncertainty of the boundary between the United States and Mexico, being acquiesced in, he, General Gaines, is authorized to cross the Sabine river, and proceed as far as Nacogdoches, 75 miles within the Mexican territory. This permission is given, however, only under certain contingencies; (and I am certain that these have not been present.) Here I must be permitted to ask, (and I address myself to every American who loves his country, and is proud of it,) how it can be maintained, under any pretext that honor would suggest, or justify, that the frontier between the United States and Mexico is *uncertain?* For a long time after the acquisition of Louisiana, the United States exercised jurisdiction only to the Rio Hondo but six miles west of Nachitoches, the intermediate territory between this point and the Sabine river, about 40 miles, being considered neutral territory. At last General Wilkinson, for the United States, and General Ferrara, for Mexico, arranged the Sabine as the frontier; a survey made by Mr. Melish also establishes the Sabine, *at this point*, as the frontier. A subsequent regular and formal treaty between the two governments confirms this frontier, and has especial and particular reference to Melish's map and survey; and more recently still, the present executive declares by proclamation, that the two governments shall continue to exercise jurisdiction within the territory now occupied by either. This was the result of a conference with the Mexican minister, who justly represented that Arkansas had overleaped the boundary between the two governments, and was in the exercise of jurisdiction within a part of the Mexican dominions.

There is certainly a part of the boundary not yet traced; but it is a line passing over land only, and running from 32d degree of latitude on the Sabine, due North to Red River. Thus it will be perceived, that all the Sabine, from the sea to the 32d degree, is the boundary; and that the Sabine above the 32d degree, belongs exclusively to Mexico;—hence the impossibility of there being uncertainty about it. I will ask again, if there is doubt as to the Sabine frontier, how it happens that when the Texans were petitioning congress for a recognition of their independence, no information was imparted to the national legislature of the circumstances.—Again, if there is a doubt as to the Sabine frontier, how happens it that war in that territory, by regularly organized armies of citizens of the United States, is tolerated against a friendly power? No, sir, there is no doubt or uncertainty as to the Sabine frontier. Mr. Secretary Cass cannot be *au fait*, or he is willing to lend himself for a most unworthy purpose.

General Gaines having, however, persuaded the Executive and Secretary that the line was "imaginary," and that he "might cross it," orders troops from forts Towson and Gibson, to occupy Nacogdoches, as I have said before, seventy-five miles beyond the limits of Mexico; and, what is worse, directs those troops to cross the Red river above, and march through the country to the place of destination; so that the troops came into the Mexican dominions at least two hundred miles beyond Nacogdoches, and, having arrived there, are ordered to fortify and erect other buildings. How is this, gentlemen? Call you all this neutrality?

But, for a farther description of our affairs here, I will add the following facts. The Americans (I mean the regulars) and Texans appear to understand each other perfectly. The neutrality is preserved on the part of General Gaines, by allowing all volunteers, and other organized corps, destined for Texas, to pass in hundreds and thousands undisturbed, but keeps in check any attempt on the part of the native Mexicans, and Indians, to act against the Texans. The Texans are allowed to wage war against a friendly power, in a district of country claimed by the United States The prisoners of war taken by the Texans are ignorant to which party they are subject. The American general claims the country only from Mexico, but has no objections to the carrying on of war against Mexico in the district he claims! Pray, sir, let Americans speak honestly, and let them say whether any government has, within the last century, placed itself in so ridiculous a light?—not only ridiculous, but contemptible. Will not any honest man confess at once that General Gaines, or any authority clothing him with the discretion so indiscreetly used, would never have dreamed of the like against a government able and ready to defend itself, and punish such arrogance? What is Europe to say to this? Will not Mexico complain? And will there be no sympathy for her?"

From this and other evidence, ample and conclusive, I repeat, it is clearly manifest, that the Texas rebellion was instigated, set on foot, and almost wholly sustained, by the exertions of those concerned in slaveholding, land-speculating, &c., in the United States. The President and Gen. Gaines are both believed to be deeply interested in this splendid scheme. They are, however, *as public agents,* mere instruments in the hands of an *extensive combination of* SLAVE-HOLDERS, SLAVE-TRADERS, LAND-JOBBERS *and reckless aspirants,* composed of all parties in this country, who have resolved to wrest the territory of Texas from the Mexican Republic, for the same reason that they have despoiled the southern Indians of their lands and other property, and have driven, and are driving them, beyond the Mississippi. These functionaries have done all that they considered it expedient to do, in order to effect the unholy purpose, consistently with the idea of an "armed neutrality;" and they have even gone further, (as I have before stated,) in setting up claims to territory that does not belong to us; in misinterpreting our treaty with the Mexican Republic; as well as in sanctioning false alarms respecting Indian depredations; in order to hold forth an excuse for making a powerful diversion in favor of the marauders who are carrying on the war against Mexico.

But it could not, possibly, be supposed that the *Mexican* authorities would be blinded by the specious pretences, and all the arts of diplomacy, that were held forth by ours upon the occasion referred to.—And although the President found it expedient to retract a little —so far as to disavow the necessity for the movement of Gen. Gaines at *that particular time*—the Mexican Envoy, at Washington, deemed it proper to break off his official intercourse with our Government, and also to enter his formal protest against its doings. This able document was immediately published, as follows:—

[Translation.]

"NOTE OF MR. GOROSTIZA,

To the Department of State.

The undersigned, &c. has learned with the most profound regret, by the note of the 13th instant, which he has just received from the Hon. Asbury Dickens, that the President, reasoning solely upon the principle of self defence, did not think that he ought to attend to the just reclamations of the undersigned, on the violation of the Mexican territory by the troops under General Gaines; and that, on the contrary, he persists in his intentions to assert the right which in his opinion he possesses, to continue violating it whenever he may deem it conducive to the better protection of the frontier of the United States.

It is obvious that the undersigned cannot, for a single moment, admit the existence of such a right; because this would be tantamount to the acknowledgment that every nation possessed it, for occupying, in a military manner, the territory of its neighbors, with no other reason than that of creating to itself an apparent necessity to act in this way; and because, on the other hand, such a right would be a continued threat to the sovereignty and independence of all of them. In fact what nation would not endeavor to fortify its own at the expense of a neighbor's frontier, if, to establish the lawfulness of the proceeding it were only necessary to assert the right.

It is obvious likewise that the undersigned cannot assent to the latitude given by the President of the United States to the principle of self-defence, when applied by him to the present case. This principle would not certainly exist, if it were not built as it is, upon justice and reason; if it were not derived, like all the other principles which together form what is called the Law of Nations, from that natural law styled by the ancients the Law of God, and which in the same manner as it imposes upon us the obligation of preserving and defending ourselves, forbids us to do so to the evident injury of a third, unless through absolute necessity, and the danger be imminent, or infinitely superior to the harm we are preparing to inflict. And, can it be said that the violation of the Mexican territory has been produced by a necessity of that nature, with its three inseparable conditions? The undersigned has not yet seen any thing to make him believe so.

What the undersigned has seen is, that the premeditated hostilities by the Indians against the frontiers of the United States, have never had existence anywhere but in the imagination of the Texians and their supporters; in other words, that they are mere inventions of the same, without any other foundation than the wicked wish of doing evil to Mexico. The simple relation of facts will suffice to demonstrate this assertion. Whilst the Texian settlers remained subject to the laws of Mexico, there was never any apprehension that those Indians wished to wage hostilities against the United States, although there had been no Mexican soldier in Nacogdoches since the year 1832, nor in any other spot near to the frontier; neither was there any talk of Indians, during the entire period of the rebellion of Texas, either before or after the taking of Bejar by the Texians. The month of March arrived, however, and the Mexican army, everywhere victorious at that time, crossed the river Brazos. No one doubted then that it would soon reach the Sabine, and it was then for the first time supposed, that fifteen hundred Indians and Mexicans were already within a few miles of Nacogdoches, putting every thing to fire and sword, in order to determine Gen. Gaines to commit so gross an imposition as to approach that very Sabine river, as he actually did. But, with the battle of San Jacinto the danger to the Texians vanished, and in their turn the Indians vanished likewise. General Gaines, who a few days before required thousands of mounted riflemen, to be able to fight an enemy whom he supposed still more formidable, then acknowledged that the alarm had been a false one, and that he no longer stood in need of such reinforcements. The calm therefore continued as long as the confidence prevailed in Texas, that the Mexican government would sanction the treaty that force alone could have compelled General Santa Anna to sign. But about the end of June, it became known that Mexico was preparing for a new campaign, and, as if by enchantment, the Indian aggressors again started up, according to what was written by the Texian Commissioners, who had gone to Matamoras to exchange prisoners; according to what the Texian General Rusk communicated afterwards to General Gaines; according to the information given to the latter by other Texian individuals; and according to the information given to the said General by the Texian Major Sterling C. Robertson, alluding to the murder of two white persons on the Navasota. It is also from that very date since General Gaines has thought he stood in need, in order to oppose the *principal belligerent*, of those very mounted riflemen which he discharged after the battle of San Jacinto,—it is since then that the defence of the frontier of the United States has required the occupation of Nacogdoches, though Nacogdoches is fifty [seventy] miles distant from said frontier. Does any one wish a clearer explanation? If not, let the undersigned be informed, what evidence has General Gaines had, for taking the step which he has taken, which has not originated from the enemies of Mexico;—from the same who are interested in the United States' compromiting their neutrality upon the Texas question?

Now, if no danger has existed; if the very rumours of it, by coming from the quarter whence they came, never ought to have inspired the least apprehension; if these very rumours have been reproduced a number of times in the space of seven months, and have been as often constantly belied by facts; how came they to be believed? How could the danger ever appear *imminent?* How could it be styled *inevitable?* Where was, in short, the *absolute necessity* which has imposed the obligation of invoking on this occasion the principle of self-defence, trampling, as has been done, in its name, upon the most sacred rights of a friendly nation?

But the President, says Mr. Dickens, has had to rely upon the reports made to him by the commanding general of the frontier, and he is ready to punish him, if he has deviated a tittle from his instructions. To this the undersigned answers, in the first place, that General Gaines' partiality in favor of the Texians has been so notorious, and his credulity so great, since the command of the said frontier has been entrusted to him, that his reports ought never to have had any weight with so enlightened a man as the President of the United States—above all, after the Governor of Louisiana and General Macomb had so well delineated the character of that general, and pointed out the influences which were directing his conduct. The undersigned answers, in the second place, that the infallible punishment of General Gaines, or of any other general, who may hereafter deviate from the instructions, which he may receive from the President in the matter, can prove of no advantage to Mexico, neither can it give tranquillity to it at present, nor afterwards repair the immense injuries which have been caused already, and those which may yet be caused to it, through the abuse already made, and which may yet be made, of the discretional power which the President has deposited with the commanding general of the frontier. And, really, of what consequence can the cashiering of any of these generals be to Mexico, if through their fault the invasion of the Mexican territory has preceded?—If, by this invasion, the Texians have been inspired with greater confidence?—If by it their ranks have been augmented with thousands of volunteers, who would not have gone to Texas, had they not believed that they could depend upon the substantial aid of the soldiers of the United States?—If, finally, said invasion being prolonged or repeated, the next campaign should arrive, and then the presence alone of the United States troops in Texas is sufficient to produce embarrassments, compromises, or collisions, which may overturn the best concerted plans of the Mexican army? Mr. Dickens will agree with the undersigned, that the government of the latter cannot receive as sufficient, a guaranty which does not protect Mexico from dangers to which she is exposed, in consequence of the presence of the United States troops upon her territory.

Mr. Dickens, with such a motive, insinuates that the last instructions forwarded to General Gaines were more precise and positive, than those which had been previously communicated to him, and therefore that his successor, General Arbuckle, will be able by adhering to them, to fulfil with greater facility, the President's intentions. But if the instructions alluded to by Mr. Dickens, are the same as those contained in the President's letter of the 4th of September to General Gaines, the undersigned cannot, in this case either, be of the opinion of the Hon. Acting Secretary of State. Quite the reverse. Indeed, the undersigned finds the latter instructions a thousand fold more arbitrary than the former; those at least designated the spot where the invasion was to halt, whereas the

latter leave the commanding general at full
liberty to pursue the Indians who, in his opinion, may wish to wage hostilities against the
United States, as far as he finds them, and
afterwards to take up a position wherever he
may think proper in any part of the Mexican
territory. The President, it is true, now
charges him not to suffer himself to be deceived
by those who give him information, and to act
thus only when he obtains any moral certainty,
that the Indians are making use in any way of
the Mexican territory, to execute their projects
of aggression. But, was not General Gaines,
perchance, charged with as much on the 4th
of May and 11th of July, by Mr. Cass, Secretary
of War, in other words. It has been already
seen how much such charges have restrained
General Gaines, and how much they will re
strain any of his successors, should they, like
him, yield to the same influences, or suffer
themselves to be imposed upon by the same
machinations. And it is almost necessary that
this should happen; for all the reports received
by these commanding generals have to come
from a country at enmity with Mexico, and
must arrive disfigured by rancour and malice.

Such are the reasons why the undersigned
has always protested, since he had to reply to
the Memorandum of Mr. Forsyth of the 20th
April, against the discretional power with
which the commanding general of the frontier
had been invested. His experience of men and
affairs immediately announced to him, that such
a power would sooner or later end in consti-
tuting its possessor the arbiter of peace or war
between Mexico and the United States. And
the undersigned certainly set too high a value
on the friendship which connected the two nations, not to shudder at the idea that their relations were thenceforth going to depend on
the will or error of an only and single individual! Mr. Dickens explains and exculpates
so much confidence on the part of the United
States, by shewing that the distance at which
the President was from the theatre of war,
would not have allowed him otherwise to attend to contingencies which might daily occur.
But France was distant from the United States
when the late differences prevailed, and the
United States would not certainly have been
satisfied then, had they seen that an Admiral
of Martinique could by a single act of his
break off at his pleasure the negociations
pending between the two governments. Would
they not justly have said, that transactions of
so great a magnitude demanded a greater
share of responsibility than could be offered by
one man, though he were an admiral or a general?

Moreover, the attention of the undersigned
has been called forth by the earnest desire
which he has observed in the United States,
to occupy Nacogdoches at all hazards; and
were it not for the assurances repeatedly given
him by the Department of State, that this
measure had nothing to do with the future de-

termination of the boundaries, he confesses
that he would be at a loss what to think of
such a desire. The undersigned calls to mind,
that this very Nacogdoches has been proclaimed by the Secretary of War as the property of the United States, when he wrote to
Gen. Gaines, authorizing him to go as far as
that place. He also calls to mind, that when
Mr. Forsyth received the protest of the undersigned against so strange a pretension, he declined by order of the President, to enter into
any kind of explanations. And he has also
observed, both in the notes of that Department, and in the correspondence which has
taken place between the Secretary of War,
General Gaines, and some Governors of States,
a certain constant study not to designate the
Mexican territory lying beyond the Sabine, by
any other name than the contested territory, or
those which were equivalent; as if the actual
treaty had not put an end to the contentions
which existed with respect to boundaries,
when the line of ancient Louisiana ran between
the rivers Mermento and Carcasiu; that is, thirty
or forty miles this side of the Sabine! But the
undersigned notwithstanding repeats, that
those assurances on the nature of the movement of General Gaines, seem to him sufficient
to dwell no longer on the estimate of coinci-
dences so strange.

Such, therefore, were the considerations
which were present to the undersigned, when
he wrote his notes of the 28th of July and 4th
of August. He considered then, as he does
now, and for the same reasons, that the invasion of the Mexican territory by the troops of
the United States, was to Mexico an offence
really gratuitous, since there had been no
provocation on its part, or any lawful excuse
on that of the United States. He then also
showed evidently the enormous injuries which
ensued to Mexico, in consequence of said invasion. He then finally announced, that if the
President did not listen to reclamations so just
he would find himself under the painful necessity of retiring with his Legation extraordinary.
But the undersigned flattered himself that this
case would not arrive; because he expected
that his reasons would be weighed in the
balance of equity, and not in that of mere
convenience.

Unfortunately, it did not happen thus; and
the note of Mr. Dickens has left the undersigned without any hope whatever. The
explanations given him in the name of the President, have convinced him, besides, how little
Mexico has now to expect from the United
States, when its most sacred rights, its dearest
and most positive interests, are sacrificed before
the shadow of a danger hitherto imaginary.
Mexico is insulted and wronged, through mere
precaution.

Under circumstances so gloomy, the undersigned would be failing in his duty, were he
not to take the last step remaining to him, to
demonstrate at least that he feels, in all its

magnitude, the wrong done to his country by the United States ; declaring as he does, upon his own sole responsibility, that from this moment he considers his mission as concluded.

The undersigned, consequently, requests Mr. Dickens to be pleased to transmit to him his passports to Philadelphia, for which place he will set out to-morrow.

The undersigned also requests Mr. Dickens to have the goodness to present his respects to the President, and to return him thanks in his name, for the personal attentions for which he is indebted to him, during the time he has had the honor of being accredited near his person.

Finally, the undersigned repeats to Mr. Dickens, what he has already had the honor of expressing to him verbally, which is, that he will always bear in mind, with gratitude and esteem, the frank and noble manner in which Mr. Dickens has conducted himself towards the undersigned, in moments truly not very

agreeable, and in affairs which by their nature have been still less so.

The undersigned, Envoy Extraordinary, and Minister Plenipotentiary of the Mexican Republic, improves this occasion to renew to the Hon. Asbury Dickens, acting Secretary of State, the assurances of his most distinguished consideration.

    (Signed)   **M. E. de Gorostiza.**

To the Hon. **Asbury Dickens**, &c. &c.
         Washington, 15th Oct., 1836."

In a subsequent very minute and comprehensive exposition of the course pursued by our government, he also gives a history of the *boundary dispute,* from which I have extracted the concluding part, and insert it below. Its great length forbids the insertion of the whole. I have likewise accompanied this extract with a Map, illustrative of the boundary, which was prepared especially for the purpose, and will be found strictly correct.

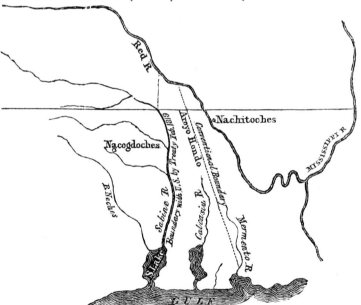

THE EXTRACT.

[Translated for the "National Enquirer."*]

"In the meantime the rebellion in Texas was increasing; and Mexico, who beheld without being able to doubt, the assistance of every kind openly rendered by the citizens of the United States to the rebels,—who observed the want of efforts on the part of the American government to counteract that assistance *effectually,*—and who perceived the sensation of dis-

pleasure which such conduct was creating necessarily in the hearts of all Mexicans, came to fear, and not without some shadow of reason, that her relations of friendship with the United States would feel the shock of so many circumstances combined to her injury, and that they would gradually cool, somewhat more than suited the interests well understood of both nations.

In order to diminish such injuries in future; in order, above all, to prevent, on the part of Mexico, any plausible motive whatever of distrust or complaint which might compromit those relations; the government of Mexico was of opinion that it ought to send to Washington an Envoy Extraordinary, who should occupy

* This very important document was translated for the *National Enquirer,* (published in Philadelphia,) and the whole of it was inserted, in that paper of December 3d, and 10th, 1836.

himself exclusively with the affairs having any connection with the questions relating to boundaries and Texas; relieving, by these means, the Charge d'Affaires already there, from the compromits of these questions, and leaving to his known zeal and efficiency the care of all the other subjects appertaining to an ordinary legation. From the appointment of said Envoy, and his going to Washington, under the circumstances of the time, two good results at least were about to be immediately derived, even if no other fruit should be reaped afterwards: the first, to manifest to the government of the United States, that Mexico still confided in its equity and amicable intentions; the second, to calm, in some degree, the public excitement, by showing the Mexicans that their government still hoped that the United States would do them justice. The American packet which arrived at Vera Cruz, last January, brought besides, amongst its correspondence, two official documents which made the Mexican government conclude in the affirmative with respect to the measure in question: one was a memorandum of a conference which Sigr. Castillo had had with the Secretary of State, at the beginning of November, in Washington; the other was the Message of President Jackson.

In that conference, Mr. Forsyth had said in the name of his government, as appeared from the Memorandum written on that day, by Sigr. Castillo, 'that the United States were resolved to defend their frontier, which they considered threatened by reason of the approaching campaign in Texas; and in order thereto, the belligerents should acknowledge as *neutral*, all that part of the Mexican territory which *might belong* to the United States, after the demarcation of limits should be made.'

And in the Message, in reference no doubt to this verbal communication, was found the following sentence: 'It has been deemed necessary to make known to the government of Mexico, that we shall require the integrity of our territory to be scrupulously respected by both parties;" without Mr. Castillo's being able to obtain from Mr. Forsyth the explanation which he desired in writing of what was really understood therein by *territory of the United States.**

Inexpressible, therefore, was the surprise of the Mexican government, on the reading of both documents, and on receiving the unforeseen and unexpected news, that a part of its actual territory, bordering upon the theatre of war, might some time or other chance to belong to the United States. This it deemed a real enigma; because how much soever it examined the past correspondence between the two governments, since the foundation of the Republic of Mexico, not a single word was to be found therein, which might indicate the existence of any claim of this kind, unless it was the cited observation of Butler, of the 21st of December, which was then disregarded as vague and unfounded; and because how often soever it read the treaty, and consulted Melish's map, which forms an integral part of the same, it was unable to perceive how any doubts could exist with respect to a territory, separated from the American territory by a running stream known by all, and un-

interrupted even for a moment in its course as high as the 32d degree. What could commissioners or geometers do in this part of the frontier, that nature had not done already? Was not the Sabine, which served as a frontier, the same Sabine which had always been?—the Sabine of the treaty of Melish,—the one ascending from the gulf,—navigable, and the same that thirteen years before the signing of the Convention of 1819, between Spain and the United States, the Dearborns and the Wilkinsons already proclaimed as such Sabine, and as such frontier? †

We repeat, that the Mexican government was at a loss to conjecture what the danger was that threatened it; but this was exactly what gave it most concern. It could not know, indeed, whether what the United States wanted, was to reap any benefit from the present difficulties in which Mexico found herself, in order to lop off a portion of her territory, or whether it was only to make a diversion in favor of the Texans; or whether they wanted both things at once; but without knowing exactly what they wanted, it could not but know that they wanted *something*, and that this *something* was always to be at the expense and to the great injury of Mexico. There was, therefore, an absolute necessity to inquire what it was, and this necessity, as we have already insinuated, at length decided the appointment of the Envoy, in such a manner that he hastened his departure for the United States, embarking at Vera Cruz on the 9th of February, and arriving in New York on the 27th. The instructions given him were. as must be presumed, numerous and various; but they all tended to the same end, that of supporting and defending the integrity of the Mexican territory, whatever might be the weapon with which it was desired to attack it, and the fraction of it which it might be intended to injure.

Scarcely had said Envoy set foot in Washington, when he was assailed by a thousand alarming reports about the security of the Mexican frontier, and when he began to collect successive data in confirmation of those reports; now, referring to what had been heard in a certain *White House*, it was repeated to him that the Sabine was not the Sabine, and that the real Sabine was the Neches; ‡ now he was assured of its having been heard from very respectable lips, that there were in Texas several rivers bearing the name Sabine; now, he was shown a periodical of the number of those which were most in the secrets and interests of the government, and was made to read therein, 'that between two different branches of the Sabine lay a wide territory claimed at once by the United States and by Mexico, and which the United States considered as their property, believing itself, therefore, under the obligation to succour and protect its inhabitants : now, he was taken to the Library of Congress, and there a manuscript map was caused to be shown to him, which had been expressly drawn for the *information of the representatives of the nation*, and in which localities and proper names

---

* Because it is really laughable to see what happens in the United States with respect to the messages of the Presidents, and what is printed in the Globe. In the former can be said any thing which occurs, or may be convenient to the President, about foreign governments, without their having to expect any other explanation than that they have nothing to do, or any concern with what has been said therein; because it was a mere domestic allocution, of a confidential character, exclusively directed to America, and only intended for them. The Globe may also insult or slander them in perfect safety, and without apprehension of compromiting the government, whose organ it is and whose confidence it possesses ; the government avoiding all responsibility by assuring that it has no official periodical, and *what has been said, remains so.*

† William Darby, the American Geographer, who in 1812, had navigated the Sabine from the 32d degree to the Mexican gulf, and who was the one that furnished Melish with all the data of this part of the frontier for his map of 1816, corrected afterwards in 1818, wrote an article communicated, under date of May 12th, 1836, in the " National Intelligencer," which completely settles the question as to the course and *identity* of said river. In this article, besides other things, Darby says: " that if when he visited that region, any one had disputed there that the Sabine was not the limit between the United States and the interior provinces, he would have been taken for a madman."

‡ The Neches is a small river of Texas, always called thus from time immemorial.   s from Lake Sabine, (not the Gulf of Mexi   arriving at 30 degrees latitude, divides into a r   ranches taking different directions, though so s   ot any one deserves to be called a river.

had been impudently falsified, in order to place the frontier on that very Neches.

On the other hand, he saw, in the seat of government, and where, excepting some senators and representatives, there is scarcely an inhabitant who does not depend directly or indirectly on the government, that there were, notwithstanding. very few who were not lively and materially interested in favor of the Texans; one, because he possessed lands purchased at a very low price, or presented to him,—another, because he speculated in slaves or warlike stores,—another, because he had some relative or friend in the ranks or administration of the Texans,—another, because he thought he would make his court better, or because he did not wish to compromit the office which he had already obtained,—another, in short, because he was a nullifier. None of these, therefore, dissembled his *sympathies*; and if any honest man in Congress, or by means of the press, dared to raise his voice in defeace of the most obvious principles of equity and law, they all fell upon him immediately, and at least called him a bad citizen, and said that he had sold himself to Mexico, or spoke in that manner because he belonged to the *opposition*.

What co ld the Mexican Envoy infer from all this? What ought he not to fear?

Notwithstanding, he still suspended his judgment, and could not persuade himself, though he *heard*, *saw*, and *read* ever so much, that the United States, who were at that momeat treating with him, precisely about the exchange of the ratification of the 2d additional article of the Treaty of Boundaries, without having insinuated to him a single word indicating discontent with its stipulations. should yet harbor already in their breast the sinister intention of violating them all —As much happened to him respectively with regard to the too great apparent protection afforded to the Texans. When the sounds still remained in his ears, of the assurances of good affection towards Mexico and of strict neutrality in the contest with Texas, assurances which he had heard from the very lips of the President of the United States, on presenting him his respects, and which had been afterwards repeated to him by all his ministers; how could he help giving them faith, so long as the least doubt remained?

But the 20th of April at last arrived, the day appointed for the exchange of the said ratifications; and hardly were the respective instruments signed, when the Secretary of State called the Mexican Envoy to a conference, and made him the communication expressed in the Memorandum bearing the date of the same day; a communication which began to tear the veil which had concealed till that time, all its ugliness of the prospect already delineated. Add to this, what the Envoy could infer from the subsequent discussions of Congress, upon the defence of the Western frontier, and other questions connected with that of Texas; questions in which the friends of the administration not only maintained in a thousand different ways, that a *contested territory* really existed west of the Sabine, but also boasted of their partiality to Texas, and enmity to Mexico:—*the degree to which his attention was called by the despatch of General Gaines of the 29th March, in which he now proposed to the President to pass with his troops the line which

* In one of them, there was a representative who, in speaking of the Envoy himself, openly called him a *skilful intriguer, and an enemy of the North Americans;* because seven years befre, neing Mexican minister in London, he alarmed the British Cabinet respecting the intentions which he already discovered in Washington, of that wanting to take possession, in some way or other, of that very territory of Texas which was now so much threatened. And does this prove any thing except that the Envoy, besides great zeal for the interests of his country, possessed likewise some small share of foresight?

he called *supposed or imaginary,*† together with the *casual and involuntary* publication of the answer of the Secretary of War. in which he had authorized him to go ' *as far as the old fort of Nacogdoches, which was within the limits of the United States as claimed by them :'*—what he was given to understand at the same time by Gaines' own letter to the governors of the four states, as it was said therein that the principal object of the projected movement was to shelter from aggression " he settlements of the whites situated on both sides of the Sabine :'—what was afterwards explained to him by the despatch of General Macomb, in which he referred to the opinion which the governor of Louisiana had of the influences which directed the said Gaines:‡—what he was afterwards to fear from the posterior conduct of Gaines himself, when he saw him, credulous and hasty, run towards the Sabine, only because some of the friends of Texas presented him some forged letters which spoke of an irruption of Mexicans and Indians upon Nacogdoches:§—what

† In the course of the Sabine as far as the 32 d degree there is certainly nothing at all supposed or imaginary; therefore it is only from the 32d degree, as far as Rio Rojo, where till now any doubts could exist, as is proved by the notorious fact, that two whole counties of Arkansas are now situated far within what will be, on that side, Mexican teritory, when the line is marked out. But Gaines neither spoke of this part of the line, nor the Secr tary of War thought of it certainly, when he told him to go to Nacogdoches, since Nacogdoches is situated 30 miles at least before arriving at the place where the Sabine ceases to be a frontier.

‡ "He (the governor of Louisiana) is persuaded besides, that it has all been a plan contrived by those interested in Texan speculations, to make Gen. Gaines believe, as they have made him believe, that the Mexican authorities were tampering with the Indians of our frontiers; and also to excite in New Orleans, by interested and slanderous advices, the sympathy of the people in behalf of the Texans, with the object of inducing the authorities of the United States, to lend their aid to raise troops of interested persons to go to the frontiers, and be under the orders of Gen. Gaines, and afterwards under false pretences to enter Texas and take part in the war between the Mexicans and Texans, all at the expense of the United States, and consequently with the supposed sanction of their government; thus inspiring the people of Texas with the hope of being able to rely on the protection and aid of the United States, and giving the government of Mexico positive evidence that the United States were at that time waging hostilities against it, with forgetfulness and in contempt of existing treaties."
See the entire despatch of Gen. Macomb in the Globe *of 16th May.*

§ One of the letters written with such an object, was the following from the so called Alcalde of Nacogdoches, who lent his aid to authorize with his signature so notorious a falsehood.—"To General Mason—Nacogdoches, April 12, 1336.—My dear sir; We hasten to inform you that the news which arrived previous to your departure is confirmed, (*the news of the appearance of 1500 Mexicans and Indians in the vicinity of Nacogdoches.)* They encamped on the Sabine night before last. They were piloted by the Caddoes. Their combined force is formidable. we being unable to affirm what it is. You know what our position is, entirely without means of defence. Many women and children will undoubtedly prove the victims of these sanguinary enemies. To-day we shall all leave this place in order to take refuge in Antognac or St. Augustin.—(Signed) B. N. Irvin, Acting Com. of this municipality."—Then follow the signatures of six witnesses who actually vouch for the correctness.

In another letter, dated April 14, Fort Jessup, addressed to the Editor of the Commercial Bulletin of New Orleans, which gives many details of this event, is seen the following paragraph.

"General Mason arrived here only last evening. and General Gaines with just promptitude ordered eight or ten companies of this garrison to march immediately to the bank of the Sabine where they will arrive to-night as soon as they can. General Gaines will assume the command of these troops, thus adding another laurel to the crown of glory which he has already acquired in the East. The trumpet of war being sounded, and the marching commenced, (*that is, the United States troops being now in motion*) the march will not cease, at least I expect so, till Mexico yields, and Texas is free. To arms, friends of a shock he must, finally, have experienced, from the unbounded joy which he perceived with astonishment in great and small, in the magnates and legislators, when the result of the battle of San Jacinto was known in Washington : let all this then, we repeat, be added to what was already alarming for the Mexican Envoy, in the contents of the Memorandum, and it will be easy to conceive what were the impressions which he was successively receiving during the first period of the correspondence now published; and how they afterwards contributed to produce his conviction for having acted in the manner that he has; even though the diplomatists of the United States may have skilfully endeavored at the last hour, to change the ground in which until then the contention had been waged, by removing to another which, if not less offensive to the dignity, rights and interests of Mexico, is at least more plausible, especially in the eyes of the American public.

A part of this correspondence has already been printed by order of the Senate of the United States, and consequently no inconvenience whatever is felt, neither is any apprehension entertained of failing in diplomatic delicacy by concluding the publication of what was written subsequently; the more so as it all turns upon a negotiation already terminated, and which, therefore, has already entered into the dominion of history. For a contrary reason, we have abstained from giving to the press, many notes relating to other Texan affairs, even though they would undoubtedly have contributed to throw much light upon the subject of the *passage of the Sabine.* We hope that the government of Mexico will order, at the proper time, the publication of all these documents, if it should ever prove useful to it to have it known, what has been till now to Mexico, the so much proclaimed *neutrality of the United States in the war which a friendly and neighbouring power has had to sustain against the ungrateful foreigners whom she had admitted into one of her most fertile provinces.* And these foreigners are all North Americans, as have been all who have aided them with their persons, money, writings, advice, and hatred towards Mexico ! ! !*

Texas, and let the volunteers of Florida on their return embark in the steamboats, and come to protect these unfortunate inhabitants, &c. &c." *Both these contemptible papers were published by the Globe, on the 4th May,* with the same air of confidence, as if it had published two documents most worthy of credit.

* This does not mean that there are not in the United States, many citizens who sincerely lament what h::s passed and is passing in their country by reason of the rebellion of Texas, and who do not *almost* wish for the triumph of Mexico out of mere respect to justice and equity; quite the contrary, there is scarcely a respectable merchant, or independent gentlemen, or a naval officer in the army or navy, or conductor of a periodical entertaining self-respect, or any functionary *who cannot be removed,* or in fine any American of the school of Washington or Madison, who does not belong to this number. But, what can so small a fraction do against the torrent of a mass necessarily ignorant, who is all powerful, and suffers itself to be blindly led by the way that suits their immoral and greedy flatterers, devoid of all principle, and consequently without any barrier to check them. Nothing, unfortunately for Mexico, and unfortunately likewise for the United States. The Mexican Envoy, however, will never forget the testimonials of sincere interest which he has observed in all those citizens, for the cause which he was charged to defend, particularly in excellent and enlightened Philadelphia, in Boston, Baltimore, and even in New York, notwithstanding this last city was the head quarters of the speculators in Texan lands. He also improves this opportunity to thank the Editors of the Nation l Intelligencer, the Atlas, the N. York American, &c. &c. for their noble efforts, and the talent with which they have defended the same cause, with no other object than that of enlightening public opinion in a matter so greatly affecting the reputation of their soil, and without the Envoy's having at least had the pleasure of knowing even by sight any of the said gentlemen.

The following extract from a "Manifesto" of the Mexican Congress, issued on the 29th of July, 1836, will show what were the views and feelings of their Statesmen, at that time, in regard to the colonists in Texas, and their insurgent allies, as well as the government of the United States. It will also exhibit the determination of that body, to maintain the honor and the integrity of the Mexican Republic, at all hazards. A combination of adverse circumstances, alone, prevented them from speedily effecting the suppression of the insurrection. It is evident that they then placed a *confidence* in the justice of those in authority, here, which subsequent events have proven to be entirely without foundation.

"MEXICANS : This name alone embraces all that the Congress of your Representatives has to say to you to-day. This name signified primitively a great, barbarous, and superstitious nation, as all have been in their infancy, whose fate it was to be coveted, at the distance of two thousand leagues, by European avarice and ambition ; sought, found, and at length subjugated, its primitive owners remaining strangers in their own land, which was to be divided amongst its new lords, for whom, besides, they were obliged to cultivate it. It became afterwards a rich colony, extolled by its possessors ; little known, but too much envied, by the nations to whom it did not belong, and peopled by a mixed race, in which already was soon confounded and thrown together, the conquered and the conquerors.

Next came the epoch of the virility of the nation ; nature raised its irresistible voice, and felt the violence with which her designs were eluded by wishing to unite extremes that had been separated by the immense ocean, and awoke in the then colonists, the sentiment of the dignity of man, the charm of liberty, and the desire to be really masters of their own homes. They entered on the glorious contest ; they sustained it heroically for eleven years, at the end of which, justice crowned its brows. They created themselves a home, and they became their own masters. Since that time the name, Mexicans, has signified a nation, sovereign and independent, that rules its own destiny, and occupies among all the nations of the globe, the distinguished rank which merits its natural advantages and the efforts which it has made to obtain it.

This sign of our eternal glory, is, that which is on the eve of being lost, and that which ungrateful and perverse persons wish to exclude for ever, substituting in its stead that of abjection and of inexplicable ignominy.

Yes, countrymen, such is the tendency of the contest in which perversity and the blackest ingratitude has engulphed you. There is no medium : for you triumph and your name will continue to signify free men, lords of their land and of themselves, or that which to-day is a respected nation, will become a degraded branch grafted on a foreign trunk, in which even its proper name will be lost. Such is the alternative, such the plans of your enemies, such your future destiny : choose.

Never have you engaged in a more noble contest, and in which decision ought to be more invariable. Until now you have contended either with your brothers or with your fathers. Falling on any of these occasions, you would have remained in the hands of your own ; you lost the end to which you aspired, not that which you then possessed, you did not gain, but your honor received no stain, for that sufficed your efforts. Had we not succeeded in obtaining our independence, nations nevertheless would have respected us, and our glory and that of our heroes would have been noted, as having fought with justice on our side ; we should have continued a Spanish colony, but feared by Spain, praised and respected by other nations. It is not so in the present contest: here you contend with foreign ingrates, with perfidious adventurers, who wish to take from us the soil on which we were born ; wrench from us the country we have conquered ; give to oblivion the name that expresses our glory, degrading us in the eyes of the universe by subjugating us, and presenting us to the world as unworthy of forming a nation, incapable of governing ourselves, and of sustaining the dignity of independent men.

It is not only necessary that these proud foreigners should not triumph : that alone of triumphing over them, and bringing them back to the order they have violated, would cause us to lose all those inestimable treasures. They have conceived the iniquitous project, and they vaunt themselves to obtain very soon, and without resistance, the possession of our territory from the Atlantic to the Pacific; to incorporate our Republic in what they call theirs; and hereafter, by right of conquest, or farther on, placing in our sight, and in immediate contact as a focus of eternal revolution for the few provinces they leave us, in which they will meet restless and denaturalized minds, of which there are unfortunately so many among us, a constant seduction of which to take advantage, and a firm prop with which to keep us in a continual uneasiness, weakening us every time more and more, until we fall by inanition into the mouth of this new dragon that will be forever open. This second mode of destroying us by dint of time, would have an infallible effect, though they would not extend at present their usurpation on other points of the Mexican territory, so that they are permitted to be independent in that of Texas. With this alone we ought to take leave forever, of all order and peace in our Republic. From thence would spring seduction; from thence, resources for conspiracies; from thence, destructive immorality; from thence, finally, would proceed the torch of discord, with which the Republic would be reduced to ashes. If the colonists of Texas are to be in-

dependent of Mexico, let the latter take leave of independence also, and conform itself to the full of becoming again a degraded colony.

Never, then, has a war more just or more truly national presented itself, a war that affects more our dignity and our honor, and that more nearly compromises our political existence. Incautious, and in good faith, we opened our arms and unfolded our bosoms to nurture those whom the unsheltered state and perhaps immoral conduct and even crimes, kept exiled from other countries. We received them hospitably in the most fertile part of our territory; we conceded to them immunities and privileges of all kinds; we even permitted them to insult humanity, making it wretched under the weight of slavery; we left them perfect liberty in their municipal government, and we only asked from them unity with benefactors in the general government; but no sooner warmed by our shelter did they recover life, than they found the means of plunging in our bosom the venomous bite in order to devour us.—Not contented with the enjoyment nor satisfied with the dignity of citizenship with us, they resolve, at whatever cost, to be our lords, subjecting us to their caprices, imposing upon us their religion, and giving us their laws.

And who are they that have formed such a design? Men without faith, without country, without other tie than that of ambition; born in different lands; differing in points of religion, education, and in habits; exiles from the countries which gave them birth, and which were too small to contain them; men unaccustomed to the hardships of war, to whom military armor is in itself weighty and embarrassing, and who perhaps tremble and turn away their heads in giving impulse to the fire and detonation of their guns; men, in fine, by no means formed for strict military obedience, inexpert in the difficult science of governing, and to whom all is contemptible excepting perversity and malice. Do not believe that the majority is composed of industrious people, anxious to moisten the ground with the sweat of their brow, and who wish no other recompense for their labor but that of the abundant harvest with which Nature would compensate them in these fertile lands; no: your enemies are divided into two classes—disheartened slaves, oppressed and deceived, and lordly, ambitious dominators. What can be hoped, or what is to be feared, from such people?—And will these give their laws to the noble, generous, and free Mexicans?

In vain have they tried to disguise their perverse intentions, and cover their ingratitude by a change in the form of government, for which the generality of the nation has decided. In vain do they profess their love for the ancient *federal* system:—were they quiet while they had it? Do their revolutionary intentions date from that time? On the contrary: has there been any time since the year 1824, in which they have ceased to give anxiety, to call the attention, and to keep the rest of the Republic in more or less alarm?

When this demonstration of facts is undeniable, what right have these new-coming adventurers to try to subject the immense majority of the nation to their caprices, or their good or bad opinions? If they once formed part of this nation, it was not by a *natural right*, but by a generous gift, of this same nation. In virtue of it they were received, and they were received *conditionally*. It was told them, 'you will have a home, country, liberty to work; we will give you lands to cultivate, and their fruits you may enjoy; we will respect your natural rights, and will concede you our civil ones; but all on condition that you will subject yourselves to our laws, obey the supreme government, and will not disturb the union and tranquillity of the people who foster you.' Did they ever comply with so just, so necessary a *condition?* Soon they became unworthy of the gift, and they deprived themselves of rights that never were other than *conditional.*—Of any other department whatever, notwithstanding the natural right of land of which they were possessed, none have the wish to subject others to their caprices; on the contrary, only the obligation of yielding to the National majority is expressed. What appearance of reason and authority have these aliens to give the slightest shade of legitimacy to their revolt? '*The same right that had America to create itself independent of Spain,*' they dare, with some other perverse revolutionaries, to exclaim in its behalf!!! Ignorant and barbarous beings! Let them assign in the archives of nature, one alone of the irresistible titles on which was founded the right of emancipation of the Americans. These were masters of their land, because on it they were born, and to it they were destined by the supreme arbiter of the whole Universe: *masters*, because they inherited it from their mothers and grandmothers; *masters*, because from their cradle they have cultivated it with their hands, watered it with their tears and sweat, making it fertile and productive; *masters*, even through respect to their parents, since they had arrived at the age of virility; *masters*, above all, *of the soil and of themselves*, because the infallible finger of Nature had marked the indestructible limits of separation, interposing between the Metropolis and the Colony two thousand leagues of ocean, and making by the same, incompatible with union and dependence, the felicity and well being of this immense people. This is the primordial object of all human societies, to which ought to be directed all means, and from which removed all obstacles. Where are in the Colonists of Texas these *natural* titles to the right of soil that our innocent generosity gave them? Where the impossibility of being happy? But why tire ourselves in parrying revolutionary phrases that could only be derived from the greatest igno-

rance, or more surely from undissimulated bad faith, desirous only of seducing and dazzling.

There is no less temerity and falsehood in the calculation of the resources in which they confide, and of the support on which these new comers appear to pride themselves. They boast of being countenanced by the government and respectable people of the United States of North America, and publicly divulge that they patronize their revolution and their views: atrocious injury to a nation reputed to be just, wise, and that proves how to calculate its proper interests. How can it be possible that this circumspect republic trampling on the faith of treaties and all the principles acknowledged as sacred by the right of nations should lend its hand to revolutionary subjects to assassinate their faithful friends?' In spite of our situation having been identical to their own, and our contest with Spain in every light just, with what cautious prudence, with what impartiality, in fact, did this nation not act towards us? What help did it give us? What succour either of arms or men, or of any other kind? They contented themselves with forming secret votes in their hearts in favor of our liberty and justice, but respecting their treaties of amity with Spain, and still more the inviolable principles of the rights of nations, they saw us combat, and they left us to fight alone. They desired our triumph, but they knew that no nation is entitled to create itself an arbiter, or to meddle in the domestic dissentions of others: that to violate this principle, or any other of those of eternal justice, is to endanger their own existence, renouncing the right of its conservation and authorising others to revolutionize their subjects, and introduce amongst them the cancer of disunion, the infallible precursor of death. She knew, that *harm* could only be done to the enemy, and even that to a certain degree either to indemnify or place her on her guard and no more; but to act so towards friends, is the blackest of infamy. It is a crime that heaven never leaves unpunished. They knew that the violation of treaties and every other injustice, was always punished sooner or later by nations; and if the shortness of man's life is such that visible chastisement finds him already in the tomb, and that the sword strikes on the stone, the long life of nations, on the contrary, more certainly invites retribution for the bitter evils they have caused. How then, could they even imagine that this nation, so circumspect in those times in which they could have been disculpated in acting in conformity to their just wishes, would now aid the factious and encourage the wicked, in violation of the solemn treaties of friendship which unite them to us?

Could it, besides, have so little foresight in its politics, not to perceive the alarm of other nations, in the concession of an intent which so greatly injures its commerce, and threatens its peace and its existence? If at some day (which is the delirious calculation of the revolters,) all the extensive American Continent were to form one Republic, one nation, the European commerce would see, in this case, lost to her forever this emporium: the Anglo Americans, would exercise an insuperable *monopoly*, furnishing the interior with the products of their manufacturing States, and the immense colossus formed on this side of the Atlantic, threatening incessantly to place one of his feet on the other shore and absorb the empires and kingdoms of Europe, carrying in one hand its seducing example, and in the other its immeasurable power. Would the powers of Europe then see with indifference this anticipated co-operation with the United States of the North! Would they not guard and protect themselves from this evil and danger?

Even though it were not so, as your Congress believes, and that by one of those vertigos that a wise Providence sometimes permits to wander through nations, these rebellious colonists had in truth found the support of which they boast, what have you to fear. The contest will be longer and more bloody, but the result is not doubtful, and would be more glorious. Are you ignorant, perchance, of what history gives credit, of all nations of the universe, that which you, yourselves are the signal example? The people who are possessed of their dignity, who know the value of their liberty, and resolve firmly to preserve it, having justice for its base, are invincible." To the happiness of a people, as connected with the reason and justice of their cause, may sometimes occur similar obscurations as to the sun; dense clouds seclude it in such a manner that it seems not to exist; but if winds brought them, the same or others will soon dissipate them, and the planet will appear again in all its immutable brightness."

The merits of the Texian Insurrection appear to have been well understood in Europe, at this stage of the contest. At a meeting in Edinburg, the following proceedings took place.—

From the Edinburg Scotsman.

"WAR IN TEXAS.

For the Establishment and Perpetuation of Slavery and the Slave Trade.

At a public meeting of the Inhabitants of Edinburg, held in the Waterloo Rooms, Friday the 30th December 1836.

The Right Honorable the Lord Provost in the Chair.

After an Address from George Thompson, Esq., the following Resolutions, moved by R. K. Greville, LL D., and seconded by Rev. Christopher Anderson, were adopted by acclamation—

I.—That Slavery and the commerce in human beings, wherever they exist on the face of the earth, are a violation of the natural rights of the species, and flagrant crimes against God; and that it is the solemn duty of every Christian community to use all proper means for their immediate, complete and universal extinction.

II.—That this meeting are of opinion that the present struggle in Texas against the Government of Mexico, is not a struggle against tyranny and oppression for the maintenance of the principles of political and religious liberty, but a civil war for the establishment and perpetuation of Slavery and the Slave Trade.

III.—That whereas the ninth section of the Constitution recently adopted by the Revolutionists of Texas, contains the following provisions:—viz.

'All persons of color, who were slaves for life previous to their emigration to Texas, and who are now held in bondage, shall remain in the like state of servitude, provided the said slave shall be the *bona fide* property of the person so holding said slave as aforesaid. Congress shall pass no laws to prohibit emigrants from the United States of America from bringing their slaves into the Republic with them, and holding them by the same tenure by which such slaves were held in the United States; nor shall Congress have power to emancipate slaves; nor shall any slaveholder be allowed to emancipate his or her slave or slaves without the consent of the Congress, unless he or she shall send his or her slave or slaves without the limits of the Republic. No free person of African descent, either in whole or in part, shall be permitted to reside permanently in the Republic without the consent of Congress.' &c. Therefore,

Resolved, That the words now cited, are, in their tendency, subversive of the liberty and happiness of the human race: in violation of the plainest requirements of the Divine Law: and opposed to the spirit of the Gospel, which declares that 'God hath made of one blood all nations of men for to dwell on all the face of the earth,'—that they are regarded by this Meeting as a disgrace to a convention of civilized men, and deserving the unmitigated condemnation of the friends of freedom and religion throughout the world.

IV.—*Resolved*, That while this meeting deeply regrets the fact, that in the United States there is a general sympathy manifested towards the Texians, it at the same time rejoices in the knowledge that there is also a large proportion of virtuous, enlightened, and Christian-minded citizens, who are labouring to avert the additional disgrace and guilt which the annexation of Texas would bring upon their country,—that it cordially sympathizes with them in their efforts, earnestly desires their success, and would invoke the Divine blessing upon all their endeavors for the freedom and elevation of the colored race.

Moved by Rev. W. L. Alexander, seconded by John Wigham, jr., Esq., that the cordial thanks of this meeting are due, and are hereby tendered, to the Right Hon. the Lord Provost, for his uniform devotion to the cause of humanity, and his conduct in the Chair on the present occasion.

(Signed)   JAMES SPITTAL, L. P.

Let us now hear the sentiments of a few more of our own public and influential characters, who have raised their voices against the interference of the United States in the contest between Mexico and the insurgents of Texas.

The following is an extract from a Speech of the Hon. WILLIAM B. REED, in the House of Representatives of the State of Pennsylvania, June 11th, 1836. He takes a more just and comprehensive view of the subject than many others had done before him.

"In the south-west there is a community struggling into independent existence, in whose behalf all the generous sympathies of this country are excited. (He referred to Texas.) If the swords of the Texians should win for them an existence independent of Mexico, it must necessarily be so precarious, that application for admission into our Union would follow as a measure of necessary self-defence. One of the complaints made by the Texians is, that the Mexican government will not permit the introduction of slaves, and one of the first fruits of independence and secure liberty (unnatural as is the paradox) will be the extension of slavery, and both the domestic and foreign slave trade, over the limits of a territory large enough to form five states as large as Pennsylvania. Such being the result, what becomes of any real or imaginary balance between the South and the North, the slaveholding and non-slaveholding interests. Five or more slaveholding states, with their additional representation, thoroughly imbued with southern feeling, thoroughly attached to what the South Carolina resolutions, now before us, call "the patriarchal institution of domestic slavery," added to the Union, and where is the security of the North and of the interests of free labor?—These are questions worth considering—the more so, as the war fever which is now burning in the veins of this community, and exhibiting itself in all the usual unreflecting expressions of sympathy and resentment, has disturbed the judgment of the nation, and distorted every notion of right and wrong. Let the Texians win independence as they can. That is their affair, not ours. But let no statesman that loves his country, think of admitting such an increment of slaveholding population into this Union. He (Mr. R.) could not but fear that there was a deep laid plan to admit Texas into the Union, with a view to an increase of slaveholding representation in Congress, and while he viewed it, in connexion with the growing indifference perceptible in some quarters, he could not but feel melancholy forebodings.

Mr. Reed said, he had referred to this subject of Texas incidentally, as forming one of those unpropitious omens to which he had alluded. That he might not be supposed to do injustice to the South, or to exaggerate the apprehended danger of the North, he would read to the House, as a partial expression of feeling on this question, extracts from influential Southern papers, which he found in a very able series of essays on the subject of Texas, recently published in Philadelphia."

Even the Hon. G. M'DUFFIE, late Governor of South Carolina, entertained very different views from the great mass of the slaveholders, and opposed the idea of countenancing the in-

surgents by the official sanction of our government. The following is an extract from his Message to the Legislature of the State, in 1836.—

"Entertaining these opinions, I have looked with very deep concern, not unmingled with regret, upon the occurrences which have taken place during the present year, in various parts of the United States, relative to the civil war which is still in progress, between the Republic of Mexico and one of her revolted Provinces.

It is true that no country can be responsible for the sympathies of its citizens; but I am nevertheless utterly at a loss to perceive what title either of the parties to this controversy can have to the sympathies of the American people. If it be alleged that the insurgents of Texas are emigrants from the United States, it is obvious to reply, that by their voluntary expatriation—under whatever circumstances of adventure, of speculation, of honor, or of infamy, they have forfeited all claim to our fraternal regard. If it be even true that they have left a land of freedom for a land of despotism, they have done it with their eyes open, and deserve their destiny. There is but too much reason to believe that many of them have gone as mere adventurers, speculating upon the chances of establishing an independent government in Texas, and of seizing that immense and fertile domain by the title of the sword. But be this as it may, when they became citizens of Mexico, they became subject to the constitution and laws of that country; and whatever changes the Mexican people may have since made in that Constitution and these laws, they are matters with which foreign States can have no concern, and of which they have no right to take cognizance. I trust, therefore, that the State of South Carolina will give no countenance, direct or indirect, open or concealed, to any acts which may compromit the neutrality of the United States, or bring into question their plighted faith. Justice—stern and unbending justice—in our intercourse with other States, would be paramount to all the considerations of mere expediency, even if it were possible that these could be separated. But they cannot.—Justice is the highest expediency, and I am sure South Carolina is the last state in the Union that would knowingly violate this sacred canon of political morality.

If any consideration could add to the intrinsic weight of these high inducements to abstain from any species of interference with the domestic affairs of a neighboring and friendly State, it would be the tremendous retribution to which we are so peculiarly exposed on our South Western frontier, from measures of retaliation.

Should Mexico declare war against the United States, and aided by some great European power, hoist the standard of servile insurrection in Louisiana and the neighboring States; how deep would be our self-reproaches in reflecting that these atrocious proceedings, received even a colorable apology from our example, or from the unlawful conduct of our own citizens!

There is one question, connected with this controversy, of a definite character, upon which it may be proper that you should express an opinion. You are, doubtless, aware that the people of Texas, by an almost unanimous vote, have expressed their desire to be admitted into our Confederacy, and application will probably be made to Congress for that purpose. In my opinion, Congress ought not even to entertain such a proposition in the present state of the controversy. If we admit Texas into our Union, while Mexico is still waging war against that Province, with a view to re-establish her supremacy over it, we shall, by *the very act* itself, make ourselves a party to the war. Nor can we take this step, without incurring this heavy responsibility, until Mexico herself shall recognise the independence of her revolted Province.

We have no official information of the precise state of our relations with Mexico. Enough is known, however, to satisfy us that the conjuncture is eminently critical. Let us be scrupulously careful that we do nothing to countenance, and all we can to prevent the calamity of a war. We are now engaged in a fearful and doubtful struggle to reform our federal system of government, by throwing off the corruptions under which it is rapidly sinking.

In this state of things, a war with any country would be the greatest of calamities; for we could scarcely hope to come out of it with anything but the mere wreck of a free constitution, and the external forms of a free government."

It will here be seen, that Gov. M'Duffie is more foresighted than the major part of his southern compatriots:—or, rather, he is not quite so reckless of the consequences of this vile crusade, as many of them are.—But his admonitions seemed to have little weight, in this case, with them. A committee of the same Legislature that he thus addressed, of which General Hamilton was chairman, made an elaborate Report, differing with him in the expediency of countenancing the insurgents, and strongly recommending encouragement from the United States. Some of the most prominent public men, in that state, expressed their approbation of the monstrous scheme of aggression.

The sentiments of the Hon. JOHN QUINCY ADAMS, one of the most able and independent Legislators and constitutional Lawgivers of this or any other nation, have been stated in the preceding pages.—Let us, however, hear the opinion of another celebrated American statesman, upon this subject.

At a large public meeting, in New York, the Hon. DANIEL WEBSTER made the following appropriate remarks:

"But it cannot be disguised, gentlemen, that a desire, or an intention, is already manifested to annex Texas to the United States. On a subject of such mighty magnitude as this, and at a moment when the public attention is drawn to it, I should feel myself wanting in candor, if I did not express my opinion; since all must suppose, that on such a question, it is impossible I should be without some opinion.

I say then, gentlemen, in all frankness, that I see objections, I think insurmountable objections, to the annexation of Texas to the United States. When the constitution was formed it is not probable that either its framers, or the people, ever looked to the admission of any states into the Union, except such as then already existed, and such as should be formed out of territories then already belonging to the United States. Fifteen years after the adoption of the constitution, however, the case of Louisiana arose. Louisiana was obtained by treaty

with France, who had recently obtained it from Spain; but the object of this acquisition, certainly was not mere extension of territory. Other great political interests were connected with it. Spain, while she possessed Louisiana, had held the mouths of the great rivers which rise in the western states, and flow into the Gulf of Mexico. She had disputed our use of these rivers, already, and with a powerful nation in possession of these outlets to the sea, it is obvious that the commerce of all the west was in danger of perpetual vexation. The command of these rivers to the sea, was therefore, the great object aimed at in the acquisition of Louisiana. But that acquisition necessarily brought territory along with it, and three states now exist, formed out of that ancient province.

A similar policy, and a similar necessity, though perhaps not entirely so urgent, led to the acquisition of Florida.

Now, no such necessity, no such policy, requires the annexation of Texas. The accession of Texas to our territory is not necessary to the full and complete enjoyment of all which we already possess. Her case, therefore, stands entirely different from that of Louisiana and Florida. There being then no necessity for extending the limits of the union, in that direction, we ought, I think, for numerous and powerful reasons, to be content with our present boundaries.

Gentlemen, we all see, that by whomsoever possessed, Texas is likely to be a slaveholding country; and I frankly avow my entire unwillingness, to do any thing which shall extend the slavery of the African race on this continent, or add other slaveholding states to the Union. When I say that I regard slavery in itself as a great moral, social, and political evil, I only use language which has been adopted by distinguished men, themselves citizens of slaveholding states. I shall do nothing, therefore, to favor or encourage its farther extension. We have slavery already among us. The constitution found it among us; it recognised it, and gave it solemn guarantees. To the full extent of these guarantees we are all bound in honor, in justice, and by the constitution.—All the stipulations contained in the constitution, in favor of the slaveholding states, which are already in the union, ought to be fulfilled, in the fulness of their spirit, and to the exactness of their letter. Slavery, as it exists in the states, is beyond the reach of Congress. It is a concern of the states themselves; they have never submitted it to Congress, and Congress has no rightful power over it. I shall concur, therefore, in no act, no measure, no menace, no indication of purpose, which shall interfere, or threaten to interfere, with the exclusive authority of the several states over the subject of slavery, as it exists within their respective limits. All this appears to me to be matter of plain and imperative duty.

But when we come to speak of admitting new states, the subject assumes an entirely

8

different aspect. Our rights and our duties are then both different.

The free states, and all the states, are then at liberty to accept, or to reject. When it is proposed to bring new members into this political partnership, the old members have a right to say on what terms such new members are to come in, and what they are to bring along with them. In my opinion, the people of the United states will not consent to bring a new, vastly extensive, and slaveholding country, large enough for half a dozen or a dozen States, into the Union. In my opinion they ought not to consent to it. Indeed I am altogether at a loss to conceive, what possible benefit any part of this country can expect to derive from such annexation. All benefit, to any part, is at least doubtful and uncertain; the objections obvious, plain, and strong. On the general question of slavery, a great portion of the community is already strongly excited. The subject has not only attracted attention as a question of politics, but it has struck a far deeper toned chord. It has arrested the religious feelings of the country; it has taken strong hold on the consciences of men. He is a rash man, indeed, little conversant with human nature, and especially has he a very erroneous estimate of the character of the people of this country, who supposes that a feeling of this kind is to be trifled with, or despised. It will assuredly cause itself to be respected. It may be reasoned with, it may be made willing, I believe it is entirely willing to fulfil all existing engagements, and all existing duties, to uphold and defend the co stitution, as it is established, with whatever regrets about some provisions, which it does actually contain. But to coerce it into silence,—to endeavor to restrain its free expression, to seek to compress and confine it, warm as it is and more heated as such endeavors would inevitably render it,—should all th s be attempted, I know nothing even in the constitution, or in the Union itself, which would not be endangered by the explosion which might follow.

I see, therefore, no political necessity for the annexation of Texas to the Union; no advantages to be derived from it; and objections to it, of a strong, and in my judgment, decisive character."

Notwithstanding all the opposition to this aggressive scheme, on the part of many of the wisest men in our country; notwithstanding the NOTORIOUS FACT, that its character, and the persons concerned in it, are precisely as I have represented; although the members of the National Legislature, as well as the Executive branch of our government, were possessed of all the necessary information to prove the reality of the monstrous iniquty attached to it; and even though the President, himself, recommended inaction for a longer time—being satisfied, from official investigation, that any interference would be premature and improper;—yet, every intelligent reader will re-

member, that a proposition for recognising this band of insurgents, as an independent nation, was made and hastily sanctioned, just at the close of the last session of Congress! Until within a *few hours* of the time when the vote was taken, no person, perhaps, anticipated such a result.—And in what manner did the usurpers thus contrive to over-reach the opponents of their unhallowed scheme?—Why, simply, by *stealing a march upon them* while they were asleep—no, WHILE THEY WERE AT DINNER!!! Even such a veteran statesman—such a long-tried and faithful sentinel as DANIEL WEBSTER, was found, "napping," or lounging away from his post, at so important a moment! According to a published statement of the proceedings, he, with several other members who were opposed to the resolution, "had not returned from dinner" when the vote was taken. True, they subsequently moved a reconsideration, but then, as time had been given to make a "dough-face" or two, the vote resulted in a *tie*, and consequently the motion was lost.

And it has ever been thus!—The slaveholders have always *ruled*, and carried every measure they wished, through the negligent supineness or the political *divisions* among the advocates of freedom and justice. The burning rebuke of John Randolph applies, with ten-fold force, in each succeeding collision between them. That sarcastic champion of slavite aristocracy told the northern politicians, long since, that they were all "afraid of their own dough-faces;"—and that as many of them could be moulded to southern patterns, at any time, as might be wanted for any purpose. Events have, so far, proved that he was correct;—and it remains to be seen, whether this state of things is to continue, in all future time, or whether THE PEOPLE of the non-slaveholding States will take the matter in hand, and inspire their representatives with political honesty, and courage, and firmness, for the faithful discharge of their solemn duties.

Immediately after the SLAVEHOLDING PARTY had thus succeeded in carrying their measures through the Senate of the United States, the President (being now relieved from all responsibility in the matter) appointed a Minister, or Charge d'Affaires, to represent this nation at the *Texian Court*. The House of Representatives appropriated the money for outfit, &c. Two Ministers Plenipotentiary were also accredited here, from that *Government*. The se ond grand step was now taken by the wholesale marauders, for the robbery and dismemberment of the Mexican Republic, and they felt confident that every thing was in proper train for its certain accomplishment. A great portion of the people in our northern Free States were still *dreaming on*, unconscious of danger, while the faithless sentinels of the Press, with a few exceptions, were themselves also asleep, or crying—"*All's well!*"

When these measures became known to the Mexican Government, the General Congress of that Republic issued the following PROTEST against them. Their Charge d' Affaires, resident in this country, was also directed to break off his intercourse with our Government,—as the Minister Plenipotentiary had previously done.

"OFFICIAL PROTEST

Of the Mexican Government against the recognition of Texian Independence.

From the Diario del Gobierno, April 10, 1837.

[Translated for the National Enquirer.]

To his Excellency, the Secretary of Foreign Relations of the United States of America. Palace of the National Government, Mexico, March 31, 1837.

The undersigned, Principal Secretary, charged with the Department of Foreign Relations of the Mexican Republic, has the honor of addressing the Secretary of the same Department of the Government of the United States of America, in order to manifest to him the just surprise, with which H. E. the President, ad interim, of this republic has seen the announcement made in the New Orleans Bee, of the 13th instant of the recognition by the Congress of the United States of the independence proclaimed by the insurgents of Texas, and of the appointment in consequence thereof, by that Government, of Mr. Alcee Labranche as their minister plenipotentiary near that of the pretended new republic.

Those steps so prematurely taken, have caused the greater amazement in the Mexican Government, as there was no reason to apprehend that such measures would have been adopted, either considering the compromises consequent to the friendship existing between the two republics, and secured by solemn treaties,—or to the assurances, contained in several official acts given by the Government of the United States, of which the undersigned takes the liberty to cite the most recent and conclusive.

When, on the 24th of May, of the year last past, Senor Gorostiza, the Minister of Mexico near the the Government of the U. S., by reason of the proposal made in the Senate, for the acknowledgment of the independence of Texas—in consequence of the reverse suffered by our troops on the 21st April—called the attention of that government to the claims of Mexico to Texas, and her means of enforcing them, the Honorable John Forsyth, Secretary of Foreign Affairs manifested to him, in answer, of the 29th of the same month, which the undersigned has before him, that he had received instructions from the President of the United States to assure him, that no decisive resolution whatever upon that question would be taken by that government unless founded upon the same rules and principles which guided it in the former disputes between Spain and the Hispano-American States: that, when all the facts were known and not before,—after a complete, impartial and careful examination, keeping in view all the considerations due to the friendly obligations existing between the two republics, that Government would proceed to decide on a question which it considered, as did the Mexican Minister, of the utmost importance in its immediate relations, and unavoidable results.

Such was precisely the language used by the Secretary at the end of May of the year last past, immediately after the only triumph obtained by the insurgents. Now let the undersigned be allowed to

ask:—Has the case supposed by Mr. Forsyth already occurred? Do the Texians find themselves, with respect to Mexico, in the position in which the Mexicans were with respect to Spain, when their independence was acknowledged by the United States? Is there any point of identity between a nation of upwards of six millions of inhabitants, who by their single efforts shook off the yoke of oppression, after a sanguinary struggle of eleven years, and cast out beyond the ocean the domineering hosts,—and some few thousands of vagrants without country, without religion, without virtues, without laws, and threatened by a numerous army, which is marching full of enthusiasm to recover the laurels denied to it by capricious fate at San Jacinto? Shall the atrocious injury be done to Mexico of supposing her so weak that, unable to vindicate her rights to the territory which those wretched adventurers have usurped from her, she should consent to the establishment of that ridiculous republic? If the undersigned were to stop to give the solution himself to these questions, he would render his note irksome by its length, and offend the known enlightened understanding of the Secretary whom he is addressing.

Another document, no less interesting than the one already mentioned, the undersigned has likewise before him. The Honorable Secretary will readily perceive that he refers to the message addressed by H. E. the President, General Jackson, to the House of Representatives, dated the 21st December, ult., on transmitting to it extracts from the report of the agent which he had appointed, and sent to learn the political, military, and civil condition of Texas, pursuant to the resolution of the two Houses of Congress, declaring that the independence of Texas should be acknowledged by that government as soon as satisfactory accounts were received that a government existed there capable of discharging the duties, and fulfilling the obligations of an independent power.

This official document, founded on the solid basis of justice and equity, and in which shine the most sublime principles of the law of nations, was published in the journals of the United States, as another additional guarantee given to Mexico that her rights would be respected. All its contents are interesting; every thing tends to ensure the neutrality of the United States in the question between Mexico and Texas. After establishing general principles, it characterizes the act of the acknowledgment of a new State as very delicate, and of great responsibility: it establishes that a premature acknowledgment, if it is not considered as a justifiable cause of war, is always subject to be looked upon as a proof of a hostile spirit towards one of the belligerent parties: it assures that every question relative to the governments of foreign nations, has always been looked upon by the United States as seditious, and that they have abstained from giving credit to them until after obtaining the clearest evidence, in order not only to decide correctly, but also to preserve their decisions from every unworthy imputation.

Descending afterwards to particular cases, it brings to mind the prudence which they observed in the controversy between Spain and her colonies, waiting not only till the capability of the new States to support themselves should be fully proved, but till every probability of their being subdued anew should have entirely disappeared: and confining itself afterwards to the question of Texas, describes the misfortune which happened at San Jacinto, and its immediate consequences; but at the same time it considers worthy of attention the resources which the government put in operation to repair it, judging consequently that, until knowing the results of the new expedition which was preparing, the independence of Texas ought to be considered as in a state of suspense. But why should the undersigned weary any longer the Honorable Secretary by making him an exposition of the contents of that official paper wi h which he must be so familiar, and which besides he has at hand in the archives of his office? It will suffice to remind him, that the President, General Jackson, was of opinion at that date, that prudence dictated to the United States to await the result—preserving the attitude kept till then—if not till Mexico or one of the great foreign powers should acknowledge the new government, at least till the process of time, or the course of events may have proved beyond a doubt, that the inhabitants of that country are able to maintain their sovereignty, and support the government established by themselves.

Now, what posterior events have occurred so powerful as to have obliged the government of the United States to give up the line of circumspect and just conduct, which it had prescribed to itself? The Mexican government is not aware of them. What guarantees are now offered by the Texans, which may be conformable to the message before cited, and so evident as to have given reason for their acknowledgment against the considerations due to a friendly and neighboring republic, and the compromises which bind the United States to her? None, certainly.

The Mexican Government deems that of the United States too just to suppose that ignoble views and purposes of aggrandizement can have induced it to take the premature step alluded to: but as it is an unquestionable fact that this step has been taken, since it has been announced in an official Journal of the United States—the Bee of New Orleans—the undersigned has received an express order from H. E. the President, ad interim, of the Mexican republic, to protest, as he does in effect protest in the most solemn manner before all civilized nations, against the acknowledgment of the independence of the pretended republic of Texas, made by the United States of America, declaring that this acknowledgment cannot in any way whatever, neither now, nor at any future time, weaken, diminish, or invalidate, in the least degree. the rights of the Mexican republic to the territory of Texas, as well as those which it unquestionably has to employ all the means that are, or may be. in her power to recover it.

The undersigned begs the Hon. Secretary of Foreign Relations, of the United States, to be pleased to communicate the contents of this note and protest to H. E. the President of the United States; and he avails himself of this opportunity to tender him his respect and distinguished consideration.

JOSE MARIA ORTIZ MONASTERIO."

The Mexicans having arranged their political matters, and elected a new President, were preparing to proceed against the insurgents in Texas again. The Government fitted out a fleet, to blockade the Texas ports, &c. &c. At THIS JUNCTURE, *our slaveholding rulers recollected,* that we have large claims against Mexico, for spoliations on our commerce!!!—And without stopping to ascertain whether Mexico had not some demands upon us, as an offset, at least sufficient to afford grounds for a little further negociation, the President forthwith despatched the following belligerent Message to Congress.—As in the case of sending the troops into Texas, under Gen. Gaines, this was a manœuvre well calculated to aid the insurgents; and it is generally known what course has since been pursued by the U. S. naval forces in the Gulf of Mexico.

" MESSAGE
Of the President to the Senate upon Mexican Affairs.

At the beginning of this session, Congress was informed that our claims upon Mexico had not been adjusted, but that notwithstanding the irritating effect upon her councils of the movement in Texas, I hoped by great forbearance to avoid the necessity of again bringing the subject of them to your notice. That hope has been disappointed. Having in vain urged upon that Government the justice of those claims, and my indispensable obligation that there should be ' no further delay in the acknowledgment, it not in the redress, of the injuries complained of,' my duty requires that the whole subject should be presented, and now is for the action of Congress, whose exclusive right it is to decide on the further measures of redress to be employed. The length of time since some of the injuries have been committed, the repeated and unavailing applications for redress, the wanton character of some of the outrages upon the property and persons of our citizens, upon the flag of the United States, independent of recent insults to this Government and people by the late Extraordinary Minister, would justify, in the eyes of all nations, immediate war. That remedy, however, should not be used by just and generous nations confiding in their strength for injuries committed, if it can be honorably avoided; and it has occurred to me, that considering the present embarrassed condition of that country, we should act both with wisdom and moderation, by giving to Mexico one more opportunity to atone for the past, before we take redress into our own hands. To avoid all misconception on the part of Mexico, as well as to protect our national character from reproach, this opportunity should be given with the avowed design and full preparation to make immediate satisfaction, if it should not be obtained on a repetition of the demand for it. To this end, I recommend that an act be passed, authorizing reprisals, and the use of the naval force of the United States by the Executive against Mexico, to enforce them, in the event of a refusal by the Mexican Government, to come to an amicable adjustment of the matters in controversy between us, upon another demand thereof made from on board one of our vessels of war on the coast of Mexico. The Documents herewith transmitted, with others sent to the House of Representatives heretofore, will enable Congress to judge of the propriety of the course pursued, and to decide upon the necessity of that now recommended.

If these views should fail to meet the concurrence of Congress, and that body be able to find in the condition of the affairs between the two countries, as disclosed by the accompanying documents, with those referred to, any well grounded reasons to hope that an adjustment of the controversy between them, can be effected without a resort to the measures I have felt it my duty to recommend, they may be assured of my co-operation in any other course that shall be deemed honorable and proper.

ANDREW JACKSON.
Washington, Feb. 6, 1837."

Although the Legislative branch of the government withheld its sanction of this Executive proposition to grant reprisals, still a squadron was immediately ordered to the Mexican coast and the capture of sundry vessels—among them a Mexican *national armed brig*—was the consequence. Again, however, our government has retracted, and censured the conduct of its officers, by restoring the captured vessel. Yet the purpose of the marauders has been effected, in a considerable degree, at least, as in the case of Gaines' invasion; and the smugglers, contraband traders, and piratical insurgents *have received convoy, protection, and encouragement, from the government of the United States.* The hope is entertained, by those interested in this unholy crusade, that such an interference may create an impression among the Mexicans to dissuade them from making further efforts to quell the insurrection, until arrangements for the annexation of Texas to the United States may receive the sanction of Congress. From the *indecent haste* already manifested, in the premature acknowledgment of its independence, it is expected that this measure, also, will be acted upon with very little further delay.

Hence, it will be seen, that the grand Marplots of Mexican aggression have, thus far, been perfectly successful in their marauding and oppressive designs. And in the confident belief that they will speedily be able to accomplish their object in full, they are said to be taking thousands of slaves into the Texas country. By a *late Decree* of the Government, these slaves will all be free, if that country remains a part of the Mexican Republic.— And the time is, probably, not far distant, when the question must be decided—whether the ADVOCATES OF FREEDOM, in Mexico, or the SUPPORTERS OF DESPOTISM AND UNIVERSAL ROBBERY, in the United States, shall be triumphant!!

It has ever been the practice of tyrants, and usurpers, to conceal their designs from the public in the commencement of their operations. The insurgents in Texas and their abettors, as I have before shown, at first merely demanded the establishment of a State Government, under the Mexican Constitution of 1824. At length, they declared for independence of all governments. And not until within a very recent period, have they, *generally*, proclaimed their *original* intention of joining the confederacy of the United States. By this clandestine course of proceeding, they lulled the people of the North into a perfect apathy, while they were secretly perfecting their measures to secure their ulterior objects. Even the lynx-eyed guardians of northern interests—the most zealous advocates of free republican principles—statesmen who had long acted as sentinels on the watch-towers of American Liberty—were all deceived by their sham professions and surreptitious policy.

But *the time has come*, when they consider it **EXPEDIENT TO THROW OFF THE MASK.** They now openly and boldly divulge their secret purposes. They frankly unfold their deep-laid plans and real objects. It is true that a few of the advocates of justice had lifted the veil of their perfidy, and exposed their ultimate designs. The eyes of many were beginning to open, and the truth was becoming visible. They are, therefore, compelled to *hasten* the consummation of their work, or all is lost. The FINAL CONFLICT is at hand.—It is "*neck or nothing*" with them now!

I have heretofore made numerous quotations, showing that it was the desire of the insurgents to annex the Texas country to the United States ; but the first public annunciation (proceeding from a responsible source) of their determination to make IMMEDIATE APPLICATION TO CONGRESS, is contained in a Report and sundry Resolutions, lately adopted by the Legislature of Mississippi. This Report is too long to copy entire ; but the following extracts embrace the substance of the whole, and present a clear view of the ground assumed for the determination expressed therein.—

" Mr. Phillips, of Madison, from the committee to whom was referred the memorial of sundry citizens of the county of Hinds, requesting the Legislature to memorialize Congress in relation to the expediency of receiving Texas into the Union, made the following report thereon, to wit:

Mr. Speaker—The select committee, to whom was referred the memorial and resolutions of sundry citizens of Hinds county, requesting the Legislature to memorialize the Congress of the United States, in relation to the expediency and necessity of receiving Texas into the Union without delay, and desiring that the Representatives of this State in Congress, and the Senators, be instructed to vote for the same, have had the same under consideration ; and having given to this highly important subject as thorough an investigation as the limited time will permit, and having duly considered the many important circumstances connected with this subject, have instructed me to make the following report as the result of their deliberations: That their decided conviction is, that the speedy annexation of Texas to this Republic is a measure highly advisable in a national point of view, and of most imperious necessity to the future safety and happiness of the Southern States of this Confederacy ; and they feel fully assured that every consideration will most completely sanction and justify this important measure.

*   *   *   *   *

In recommending the speedy annexation of Texas to the United States, the committee are influenced greatly by the following cogent reasons.

It is evident that Texas is, at present fully authorized by the laws of nations to form commercial treaties, and treaties offensive and defensive, if she choose so to do, with foreign powers. Treaties of the former kind, varying almost infinitely in their stipulations, exist between all the civilized nations of the world. Treaties of the latter kind have been frequently entered into, both in ancient and modern times; and, indeed, several of this class are now known to exist. It would be easy to imagine a commercial treaty to be effected by her with Great Britain or France, for example, which might prove highly detrimental to the commercial interests of the United States; as, for instance, a treaty by which, for a limited time or for years, commodities of British or French growth or manufactures, should be admitted into the ports of Texas free of duty in consideration of reciprocal advantages to herself. Such a treaty would have in it nothing offensive to the laws of nations; and yet it is very manifest that the amount of detriment resulting from its formation, would be very great to the revenue system, as well as to the domestic manufactures of this Republic, now asserted to need protection from congressional legislation to enable them to compete successfully with foreign fabrics. A treaty offensive or defensive, with either of the above nations, might by possibility, at some future day, afford the opportunity of conveniently introducing within our limits the embattled legions of a foreign foe, against whose assaults, were Texas a part of this Republic, we would be effectually fortified, except on our Atlantic coast and northern boundary.

*　　*　　*　　*　　*

But we hasten to suggest the importance of the annexation of Texas to this Republic upon grounds somewhat local in their complexion, but of an import infinitely grave and interesting to the people who inhabit the southern portion of this Confederacy, where it is known that a species of domestic slavery is tolerated and protected by law, whose existence is prohibited by the legal regulations of other States of this Confederacy; which system of slavery is held by all, who are familiarly acquainted with its practical effects, to be of highly beneficial influence to the country within whose limits it is permitted to exist.

The committee feel authorized to say that this system is cherished by our constituents as the very palladium of their prosperity and happiness, and whatever ignorant fanatics may elsewhere conjecture, the committee are fully assured, upon the most diligent observation and reflection on the subject, that the South does not possess within her limits a blessing with which the affections of her people are so closely entwined and so completely enfibred, and whose value is more highly appreciated, than that which we are now considering.

*　　*　　*　　*　　*

It may not be improper here to remark, that during the last session of Congress, when a Senator from Mississippi proposed the acknowledgment of Texian independence, it was found, with very few exceptions, the members of that body were ready to take ground upon it, as upon the subject of slavery itself.

With all these facts before us, we do not hesitate in believing that these feelings influenced the New England Senators, but one voting in favor of the measure; and indeed Mr. Webster has been bold enough, in a public speech delivered recently in New York, to many thousand citizens, to declare that the reason that influenced his opposition was his abhorrence to slavery in the south, and that it might, in the event of its recognition, become a slaveholding State. He also spoke of the efforts making in favor of abolition; and that being predicated upon and aided by the powerful influence of religious feeling, it would become irresistible and overwhelming.

This language, coming from so distinguished an individual as Mr. Webster, so familiar with the feelings of the North, and entertaining so high a respect for public sentiment in New England, speaks so plainly the voice of the North as not to be misunderstood.

We sincerely hope there is enough good sense and genuine love of country among our fellow countrymen of the Northern States, to secure us final justice on this subject; yet we cannot consider it safe or expedient for the people of the South to entirely disregard the efforts of the fanatics, and the opinions of such men as Mr. Webster, and others who countenance such dangerous doctrines. This unholy crusade has not only a potent band of moral agitators in our own country, but they are encouraged and stimulated to action by a hypocritical fraternity of polar philanthropists across the Atlantic, headed by the recreant and purchased champion of Ireland's wrongs, whose eyes have ceased to weep over the notorious griefs of his own countrymen, that they may more conveniently distil the tears of briny sympathy over the fancied ills which appertain to a foreign land. It is true that the President, in his inaugural address, has taken a decided stand in favor of the rights of the South; but this affords us a very precarious safeguard against the tide of fanaticism which is rapidly setting against us. The time is rapidly approximating when our northern territory, which is fast populating, will claim admission into the Union, and when those who now avow the opinion openly that the crusade that has been commenced against slavery in the South, is instigated and sustained by religious feeling, will be able to give us more serious annoyance than we have heretofore experienced.

The Northern States have no interests of their own which require any special safeguards for their defence, save only their domestic manufactures; and God knows they have already received protection from Government on a most liberal scale; under which encouragement they have improved and flourished beyond example. The South has very peculiar interests to preserve; interests already violently assailed and boldly threatened.

Your committee are fully persuaded that this protection to her best interest will be afforded by the annexation of Texas; an EQUIPOISE of influence in the halls of Congress will be secured, which will furnish us a permanent guarantee of protection.

*　　*　　*　　*　　*

It has been urged by sectional prejudice, that the recognition by the United States of Texian independence is of too recent origin to justify her immediate admission into the Confederacy. The committee confess that they can see no force, or even plausibility, in this objection. When a foreign Government has been once fairly recognised, as Texas has now been, by the United States, and even diplomatic relations having been established with her she is evidently as fully entitled to be considered, by the nation recognising her, as being fully possessed of all the attributes of national sovereignty, as it is possible for her to become at any future period; and, therefore, Texas must be deemed, by our Government, at least, as fully authorized to enter upon a treaty of annexation now, as if she had existed as an independent nation for centuries. Upon the question of recognition, every government is considered as acting absolutely on its own judgment; and when her opinion shall have once been distinctly expressed, a decent regard for her own dignity will admonish her that she is bound to act, in all respects in strict accordance with that opinion, without regard to the views or opinions of any other nation whatever. The United States having recognised the independence of Texas, is bound to consider her, in all respects, as capable at once to enter upon the work of annexation.

*　　*　　*　　*　　*

The extent of fertile soil, with salubrity of climate so remarkable in Texas, would furnish in its annexation to the Union, homes and fortunes to many of our needy citizens; with a great increase of the valuable staple exports of the country greatly augmenting our wealth, importance, and national greatness. In all the various bearings in which the committee have been able to view this important subject, they are thoroughly convinced of the expediency of the annexation as early as practicable. And in conclusion would ask leave to offer the following resolutions for the consideration of the Legislature:

Resolved, That it is expedient, in a national point of view, to comply with the desire of Texas to become an integral portion of this Confederacy without delay.

Resolved, That the annexation of Texas to this Republic is essential to the future safety and repose of the Southern States of this Confederacy.

Resolved, That our Senators in Congress be instructed, and our Representatives be requested, to use their best exertions to procure the annexation of Texas to the United States as early as practicable."

Of the public Presses, in the United States, that now openly and zealously advocate the immediate action of Congress upon this subject, the most prominent are—the "*Reformer,*" at Washington, and the "*Evening Star,*" and the "*Courier & Enquirer,*" at New York. The first named is the principal organ of the Slaveholding Party in the United States. In noticing the Report and Resolutions of the Mississippi Legislature, which I have inserted in a preceding page, the editor remarks as follows:—

"We lay before our readers the report of the Select Committee of the Legislature of Mississippi on the subject of Texian affairs. It presents a clear and forcible view of one of the most important questions which ever came before this country. The manner in which it is treated reflects great credit on the ability, patriotism, and sound sense of the chairman of the committee, Mr. Phillips of the county of Madison. He exhibits a perfect knowledge of the whole subject—a just estimate of the importance of the considerations involved—as well as of the difficulties and embarrassments that surround the question. He anticipates every objection, whether on principle, policy, or feeling, and triumphantly answers them. So thoroughly convinced was the House, of the fullness and conclusiveness of the argument, that they adopted the report and resolutions without a dissentient voice.

There is no doubt that the annexation of Texas to the Union will be distinctly and urgently pressed at the next session of Congress—and we shall see whether the love of Union is so far gone, or fanaticism so mad, as substantially to avow the principle that no farther acquisition of territory shall ever be allowed on our southern frontier, because the South tolerates domestic slavery. No one can doubt that the only objection is based on this prejudice against slavery, and terminates in a desire to maintain an unjust preponderance of political power. Such an objection cannot obtain but by disregarding totally

every principle that led to and sustains the Union of the States. The South cannot admit it—cannot countenance it for a moment, for it would divest them at once of every thing like *equality of rights under the Constitution,* and doom them and their posterity to perpetual imbecility.

It is not for us to anticipate the result. The contest will probably be violent—and though we cannot hope for much from the mad fanaticism which is abroad, we still indulge the belief that the good sense and patriotism of the Congress of the United States will triumph over the narrow bigotry and blind fanaticism of reckless faction. Should we be disappointed in this expectation, we shall look forward with fearful forebodings to the consequences. The question must test the patriotism of public men—for on it, we verily believe, hangs the destiny of this Union."

There can be no mistake in language so plain as this. The real *object,* in advocating the annexation of Texas, is here distinctly admitted: and comment would be altogether superfluous.

The other Presses to which I have adverted, are not less decided in their advocacy of the annexation. They represent both the interests of the slaveholders and the Texas land speculators:—and it is their business to maintain and defend their pretensions and their measures. To show their manner of reasoning—or, rather, their unprincipled mode of argument—I will present the reader with some brief extracts from one of them. The editor of the *Courier & Enquirer* has very lately published a series of essays upon the subject before us, from one of which I copy the following:—

" In our two previous numbers on the subject of Texas, we have confined ourselves first, to the justifiable causes which induced Texas to declare herself independent of Mexico; and secondly to a consideration of the effects which the admission of Texas into the Union would have upon Slavery and the Slave Trade. On this point the favorable effects are so obvious, that a gentleman who has been somewhat conspicuous as a member of the Colonization Society, called upon us and declared that he was so well satisfied that the admission of Texas would lessen both the extension and the evils of slavery, that he was no longer opposed to the measure.

But the best grounds on which the admission of Texas into the confederacy can be urged, are to be found in her position, the character of her soil, her productions, and the manners, feelings, and political principles of her people. Until Mr. Adams very unwisely concluded the Treaty for the purchase of Florida, and therein gave Spain a quit-claim of our interest in Texas, there can be no doubt but we had a legal claim to the sovereignty of the greater part of that beautiful region—a claim which might since have been amicably settled with Mexico, by the mere running of a boundary line satisfactory to both parties. But the aspect of affairs is now changed, Texas has established her independence of Mexico, and the United States have recognised her as a free, sovereign, and independent nation. She is, however, settled by people from the United States, and they having established the independence of their country, approve our government and ask to be admitted to the privileges of membership with the other sovereignties of our confederation. They have a right to make such application, and it is our right and interest to yield a prompt assent. In the exercise of such right we might give offence to Mexico; but that would be easily obviated by the payment of a fair equivalent, and no other nation would have any right to meddle with the affair.

The cotton lands of Texas are more extensive than those of the United States; they are more favorably located; and in consequence of their richness and the greater mildness of the climate, the cotton seed does not require to be annually renewed as in the United States, whereby, a very great saving accrues to the planter in its cultivation. If Texas should become a part of the Union, their cotton-fields will but add to our commerce and our wealth; but spurn her overtures for union, and she at once becomes our successful rival in the cotton markets of Europe, when she will not only be able to undersell us, but from which she will absolutely drive us within ten years! Are we of the north prepared to witness this state of things? Are we prepared to deprive ourselves of the advantages of the immense increase of our commerce which the annexation of Texas would give us? Nay, are we willing to see our present commerce destroyed by driving Texas into a union with a foreign country and giving employment to its shipping at the expense of our own? If Texas can grow cotton cheaper than the United States; and if from the extent of her cotton lands and their productiveness, she can, in ten years, raise sufficient cotton to supply the demand of Europe, will we not lose the advantage of shipping this cotton to Europe and importing its value in our shipping, and at the same time be deprived of our present valuable commerce in this article by reason of its having been driven from the foreign market by the cotton growers of Texas? Thus much for our *interest* in the admission of Texas. Now let us suppose that Texas, finding herself spurned by the United States, and in want of funds to carry on her Government until such times as her resources are developed, makes application to England for aid; and in order to induce her to grant it, not only forever gives her a preference in her ports and excludes all but her from participation in her carrying trade, but enters into a treaty of alliance offensive and defensive, by which England shall guarantee to Texas her separate independence, and Texas be bound to aid England in all her struggles on the American continent! Such an alliance is not only *possible*, but we speak advisedly when we say, it is more than *probable* if the United States refuse to receive Texas into the Union. And what would be our political position then? Would we be wise in thus placing an English province, or an English ally on our South-western border whence we might, at any time, be seriously annoyed? This subject is one full of reflections, and we think it need but be presented to the people in its most simple form, to insure from them the gravest, and at the same time, a favorable consideration. It is a question of vital importance to the *North* far more than to the *South*, and we hope to see the day arrive when our statesmen will meet this question as it should be met, and by boldly exposing the deceptions which have been practised upon the people, satisfy them that they cannot oppose the admission of Texas into the Union,

without being recreant to the best interests of the country."

I trust that every intelligent reader will now perceive that the GRAND COMBINATION, of slaveholding despots and avaricious marauders, are determined to push their daring schemes of outrageous wickedness to the extent of their power, without a moment's delay. I could multiply quotations, similar to the foregoing, but I consider it altogether unnecessary.

CITIZENS OF THE FREE STATES!—Are you prepared to sanction the acts of such freebooters and usurpers?—Nay more:—Are you willing to be MADE THE INSTRUMENTS of these wanton aggressors, in effecting their unholy purposes, and thus not only excite the sympathizing maledictions of other human powers, but also invoke the awful judgments of Heaven against you? Some of our wisest statesmen have spoken out, in condemnation of their deeds; and the *patriotic* conductors of the Press are likewise beginning to awaken the public attention to them.

You see that they are now fully resolved to make a speedy application to Congress, for the incorporation of the government which they have thus assumed into the confederation of the United States. *This will be attempted the very moment that an opportunity is presented.* PEOPLE OF THE NORTH! WILL YOU PERMIT IT?—Will you sanction the abominable outrage; involve yourselves in the deep criminality, and perhaps the horrors of war, FOR THE ESTABLISHMENT OF SLAVERY IN A LAND OF FREEDOM; and thus put your necks and the necks of your posterity under the feet of the domineering tyrants of the South, for centuries to come? The great moral and political campaign is now fairly opened. Your government has fully espoused the cause of these land-pirates and freebooters. Can you still remain silent, and thus lend your sanction to the unparalleled and Heaven daring usurpation? With deep anxiety, I await your response;—and trust it will come in the loudest tones of a thundering NEGATIVE, resounding o'er your granite mountains, and echoing through every valley north of "Mason and Dixon's Line."

You have been warned, again and again, of the deep machinations, and the wicked aggressive policy of this despotic "SLAVEHOLDING PARTY." I have unfolded i's marauding designs, and pointed out its varied plans and movements. You *would not listen* to these earnest entreaties and admonitions. You have slumbered in the arms of *political harlots*, until they have nearly shorn you of your locks, and bound you with the bloody cords prepared by the Philistine horde of tyrannical desperadoes. Arise!—ARISE QUICKLY! and burst those bands, or your doom, with that of your posterity, is sealed perhaps for ever !

A CITIZEN OF THE UNITED STATES.

CONTENTS.

————⋙✠⋘————